RESPECT

RESPECT

A Girl's Guide to Getting Respect and Dealing When Your Line Is Crossed

by Courtney Macavinta and Andrea Vander Pluym

edited by Elizabeth Verdick

illustrated by Catherine Lepage

free spirit
PUBLISHING®

Helping kids
help themselves™
since 1983

Library of Congress Cataloging-in-Publication Data
Macavinta, Courtney.
     Respect : a girl's guide to getting respect and dealing when your line is crossed / by Courtney Macavinta and Andrea Vander Pluym ; edited by Elizabeth Verdick.
          p. cm.
     Includes index.
     ISBN 1-57542-177-1
1. Teenage girls—Psychology. 2. Teenage girls—Conduct of life. 3. Respect. 4. Self-esteem in adolescence. 5. Interpersonal relations in adolescence. I. Macavinta, Courtney. II. Vander Pluym, Andrea. III. Title.
     HQ798.M23 2005
     158.1'0835'2—dc22

                                                                                    2005008375

At the time of this book's publication, all facts and figures cited are the most current available. All telephone numbers, addresses, and Web site URLs are accurate and active; all publications, organizations, Web sites, and other resources exist as described in this book; and all have been verified as of April 2005. The author and Free Spirit Publishing make no warranty or guarantee concerning the information and materials given out by organizations or content found at Web sites, and we are not responsible for any changes that occur after this book's publication. If you find an error or believe that a resource listed here is not as described, please contact Free Spirit Publishing. Parents, teachers, and other adults: We strongly urge you to monitor children's use of the Internet.

Cover and interior design: Marieka Heinlen
Editorial assistant: Sarah Fazio
Index: Ina Gravitz

10 9 8 7 6 5 4 3
Printed in the United States of America

Free Spirit Publishing Inc.
217 Fifth Avenue North, Suite 200
Minneapolis, MN 55401-1299
(612) 338-2068
help4kids@freespirit.com
www.freespirit.com

Dedication

This book is dedicated to our moms and sisters
and all the girls and women who are fighting every day
for their birthright: respect.

Acknowledgments

We are deeply grateful to the following people who helped to make this book possible:

The hundreds of girls and young women who shared their personal stories, thoughts, and advice to be included in this book—*Respect* wouldn't be what it is without your honesty and desire to help other girls.

Elizabeth Verdick, our ever-respectful and brilliant editor who has been a devoted collaborator in helping us inspire girls to get the respect they deserve. The staff at Free Spirit Publishing, creative superstar Marieka Heinlen, editorial assistant Sarah Fazio, production editor Ivy M. Palmer, and publisher Judy Galbraith, for believing in our book and helping to make it happen.

Our friends and family (especially our husbands Matt Hightower and Max Brace) for supporting us and our mission. Chicks Who Click, a power network of smart and talented women, who contributed resources, stories, and inspiration. The fabulous women who pitched in along the way and helped us shape our vision: Elizabeth "Betsy" Frankenberger, Sydelle Kramer, Tiffany Larson, Emily Oinen, Peggy Orenstein, Barbara Pollack, and Heidi Swanson.

And lastly, to all the experts and authors who generously offered us their encouragement, know-how, referrals, or research in their ongoing commitment to nurturing self-respecting girls:

Shirley Billigmeier, author, *Inner Eating*

Debora Burgard, Ph.D., founder, BodyPositive

Carrie Ellett, director of program and recruitment, Girls For A Change

Milena Esherick, Psy.D., director of the eating disorders program at El Camino Hospital, Mountain View, California

Andrea Frank Henkart and Journey Henkart, coauthors, *Cool Communication: From Conflict to Cooperation for Parents and Kids*

Sara Jones, teen program coordinator, Support for Battered Women Network, and her Students Talking About Relationships peer educators: Laura, Nick, Fred, Jared, and Veronica

Robert Jupe, M.F.T., L.C.S.W.

Larina Kase, Psy.D., MBA, psychologist at the University of Pennsylvania and president of Performance and Success Coaching

Peggy Klaus, author, *Brag! The Art of Tooting Your Own Horn Without Blowing It*

Carole Lapidos, M.S.W., founder, Raising Strong and Confident Daughters

Deborah Nagle-Burks, Ph.D., executive director, Oak Tree Bereavement Center

Nancy Niemi, assistant professor, Nazareth College Department of Education

National Women's Law Center staff

Planned Parenthood Federation of America staff

Tina Pieraccini, professor of broadcasting and mass communication, State University of New York at Oswego

Rachel Safier, author, *There Goes the Bride: Making Up Your Mind, Calling It Off and Moving On*

Whitney Smith, founder, Girls For A Change

Stu Sofield, lead instructor, Impact Bay Area

Daphne Stevens, Ph.D., L.C.S.W.

Giovanna Taormina, Girls' Circle Association

Jessica Weiner, author, *A Very Hungry Girl: How I Filled Up on Life and How You Can, Too!*

Tina Wells, managing partner, Blue Fusion

Contents

Introduction

We're going to tell you something that no one told us straight out when we were growing up: **Respect is every girl's birthright.** Yep, you're a card-carrying member of the human race, and that means you're owed respect. The thing is, you don't always get the respect you deserve—so you have to claim it. We're talking about how much respect you have for yourself and how much you're getting from others.

Over the years, we've connected directly or virtually with thousands of girls through our jobs as reporters and editors and our volunteer gigs with girls' organizations. The girls we've talked to and worked with come from all walks of life, but they have one thing in common: They've experienced disrespect. And we also know this firsthand. That's why we've made it our mission to help girls become stronger in every way so they are never held back in life.

Like many of you, we've been through traumas, dramas, and dilemmas. We admit we've made some cringe-inducing mistakes, gotten our feelings hurt too many times to count, and felt as if the world was crashing down on us. Then there were the many moments when we had no idea who we really were or wanted to be. But we weren't all trouble. Hardly! We had strengths, smarts, and talents. And we were forging paths—all on our own—toward college degrees, passionate careers, and close relationships with people we care about.

Still, looking back, we wondered why the bold women we are today weren't running the show 24/7 in our middle and high school years. Why did we have to learn so many lessons the hard way? Why did we struggle with so much self-doubt or worry about what other people thought of us? Because we didn't always have what every girl needs most on the path from girlhood to womanhood and for the rest of her life: *respect*. We weren't always giving it to others or ourselves. And we weren't always getting it from our world: family, friends, love interests, relatives, teachers, the media, society.

So, how do you get this respect we're talking about? For starters, by believing you deserve it. By getting to know yourself. By valuing your total originality—hey, there's only *one* you. By being honest about what you want, need, and think. By listening to that voice inside that says what feels right or wrong. By being a girl on a mission. By supporting other girls. And by speaking up when your line is crossed.

Figuring out who you are and what you stand for isn't as easy as taking some light-hearted magazine quiz and adding up the points. Building respect for yourself and with those around you takes time and effort, and means seeing the world in a new way. We wrote this book to help you learn how to do all of this and more. You'll learn about the steps toward respect, from taking care of your mind and body, to setting boundaries with others, to taking action to make the world a better place.

Now here we are, those former teen girls who struggled to find respect without a compass or a clue—but discovered that it was inside us all along. And here's the most important thing we learned and lived to pass on to you: By making respect an everyday item, you can deal with the past, make the most of the present, and plan for an amazing future.

When girls everywhere are feeling respect and spreading it all around, the world will be stronger for it. In the meantime, you can lead the way by becoming who you're supposed to be with respect and without apology: 100 percent you.

—Courtney & Andrea

You Talked, We Listened (and Wrote It Down)

Hundreds of girls have contributed their voices to *Respect*. From past interviews to conversations and online submissions specifically for this book, we've included the best quotes, advice, and wisdom we could fit in these pages. All of the quotes and stories are from real teen girls and young women. We've edited for length at times and have changed names to protect people's privacy. Ages reflect how old a young woman was at the time of the interview.

Part One:

Respect on the Inside

Your Rights

To make it in this world, you need respect like you need the air you breathe. Respect is connected to everything, from the choices you make, to how you feel, to who you are. Here's the main rule to remember: Every girl deserves respect. And getting it—from yourself and others—starts with knowing that you have certain rights.

You have a RIGHT to:

* Feel like you belong and are an equal

* Figure out what you need and take care of yourself

* Listen to your true feelings

* Speak your mind, change your mind, and question the world around you

* Be different from your family, your friends, and media ideals and images

* Feel and be safe

* Become independent

* Follow your passions and be the real you

1

What Respect Means to You

You're living in a time when girls and young women have more choices than ever before. Only a few generations ago, girls had lots of limitations—just ask your mom, aunts, grandmothers, or any other women you know. The great thing is, as you get older your choices continue to multiply. You have the choice to educate yourself about anything under the sun. To explore your talents and hobbies. To earn your own money. To be a world-class or just-for-fun athlete. And someday, maybe even travel the world, run for public office, or start your own business. It's your world for the taking.

With all the amazing advancements girls have made, why all this talk about respect? Because it's not just about your options, but about how others treat you and how you treat yourself. It comes down to this: The more respect you have in your life, the more you'll get out of life.

What you may not have realized is that every day you're already fighting for respect. Many girls say they feel like they can't be themselves because of

respect is . . .

Something you earn by being honest and courteous to others.—Julia, 13

People listening to what you have to say and valuing your feelings and opinions. —Deborah, 15

Having the confidence in yourself to be your very best.—Lauren, 16

Being treated in a way that lets you know that what you do or say is important in the world. —Erika, 14

Treating someone with dignity and telling the person that she is worth something.—Mya, 14

When people like you and appreciate you for who you are, not what you look like. ——Brianna, 13

When someone treats you like an equal human being, period.—Ashley, 15

gender stereotypes like "Girls are sugar and spice and everything nice." Other girls say they're under a lot of pressure to fit in and to focus on their looks. And no wonder: Television, movies, magazines, and Web sites all advertise products to improve your looks, wardrobe, and social life. Even if you don't believe the hype, you're surrounded by messages that say you have to focus on your *outside* to feel good on the inside.

In *The Body Project: An Intimate History of American Girls,* historian Joan Jacobs Brumberg shows how today's consumer-driven society has changed the way girls grow up. Many girls have made their body their "central personal project," as if the pursuit of physical perfection can lead to a better life. Today, growing up girl means that you're encouraged to be smart and independent, but at the same time, you're told to package yourself as an object of desire. No matter how much pink glitter you sprinkle on it, this message isn't our idea of girl power!

The *real* you is your mind and heart, including your ideas, dreams, and feelings. When you have self-respect, you know who you are and what you want. Understanding what respect is, and what it isn't, can change your life forever. This is the secret you'll learn throughout this book: Respect is always within reach because true respect starts on the inside. Now that's the kind of girl power you can really use in life.

The 7 Respect Basics

Respect is the difference between feeling good about yourself and being filled with self-doubt. Between being listened to and being ignored. Between doing what you want with your life and what someone else decides for you. Between a conversation and a screaming match. Between "no means no" and "no means yes."

Respect is ultimately expressed by actions and words—yours and those of the people around you. How can you get the respect you deserve and make sure your rights are honored? By learning and living these basics:

1. Having Self-Respect

"Self-respect" is defined by the dictionary editors of the world as "A proper respect for oneself as a human being." It's about taking care of yourself, because you're worth the effort. That includes listening to your feelings, figuring out what you believe in, and making choices that are right for you. When you take the time to think about what matters to you, you'll be more confident sticking up for yourself and your rights.

It helps to think of self-respect as an ensemble that's only complete with some must-have accessories:

self-worth, *n*. The sense of your own value and worth.

self-acceptance, *n*. An acceptance and appreciation of who you are, the way you are.

confidence, *n*. The belief that you can do what you set your mind to.

validation, *n*. Confirming for yourself that you and your feelings matter (and hearing it from other people).

2. Listening to Your Gut

Ever heard the saying "Go with your gut"? Inside every girl there's a voice that tells you what you really think and feel deep down. This voice (sometimes it's just a whisper) gives your body signals or gut feelings. Paying attention to those signals will help you stay in touch with your needs and fears each and every day.

Sometimes, you might ignore your gut feelings. Why? Maybe you're being pressured. Have you ever been in a situation where your friends wanted you to do something that you didn't want to do, and then you did it anyway instead of going with your gut? Or maybe the adults in your life put on the pressure. Your mom might have her heart set on seeing you perform in the school play, and even though you want to go out for the track team you end up at play tryouts instead, just to please her. When it's hard to go against what other people expect of you, you might ignore what your heart tells you. You might not listen to yourself because you want to please others, you're afraid of looking bad, or you think it'll be easier to do what's more popular or accepted.

In the end, where does ignoring your own thoughts and needs *really* leave you? For starters, you could get stuck doing things you wish you hadn't. Listening to your gut is a form of self-protection. This shows you trust the important messages coming from someone you should listen to: **you.**

3. Setting Boundaries

A boundary is a line—usually an invisible line you set that you don't want others to cross. Your boundaries are defined by your personal limits, values, and life experiences. If you're in a situation that makes you feel uncomfortable or if someone does something to you that you don't like, your line has been crossed. The boundaries you set can affect how a person talks to you, how someone treats you, how someone might touch you, and so much more.

Boundaries aren't walls that close you in or keep people out—they're more like a clear protective bubble you create around yourself. In fact, boundaries are actually about letting people in. Setting and honoring boundaries builds respect in your relationships. When you communicate your boundaries, you let people know what you're comfortable with and what will help them be closer to you.

But you can't expect people to *guess* your boundaries (or vice versa). We all have to speak up and let our boundaries be known. Usually, the best way to draw a line with someone is by using a straightforward, strong voice to say something like, "I don't feel comfortable when you _____. Please don't do that around me anymore."

4. Speaking Up

You deserve to be heard. This is important, so we'll say it again: **You deserve to be heard.** Every girl needs to say what's on her mind. When you speak up and others listen, you feel more like you truly matter (you know, that validation thing).

At times, you may have difficulty speaking up because you're afraid of being judged, or you don't think you have anything meaningful to say. Sometimes, you can be so out of touch with yourself that you're not even sure what you want to say. Speaking up—and speaking out—is about telling the truth as you know it, even at times when you don't feel confident. It takes courage to be honest about your feelings, opinions, and boundaries. But when you are, other people get a clearer idea of what you stand for—and what you won't stand for. And they learn how you want to be treated.

When you speak up, you draw attention to your mind and not your body, and it says to people, "Hey, I've got something to say!" That's a heck of a lot more self-respecting than just smiling and nodding your head. Although speaking your mind or sharing your feelings may not always come naturally, you can practice to get better at it. Learning to speak up with confidence and honesty is essential to setting boundaries and building better relationships. The more you speak up, the easier it gets.

5. Building Strong Relationships

You don't spend your days and nights alone in the same room—most of the time you're probably with other people. So, think about how you want to be treated and then tell your family, friends, and love interests what you need. Learning how to communicate respectfully is a key step in any relationship. And it starts with you.

One secret for any girl who's looking for respect is to give it to other girls, and to create strong relationships with them. Embracing other girls, accepting them for who they are, supporting each other's rights—that's what sisterhood is all about. Some people think sisterhood was just a political movement in the '60s that got lost along with peace symbols and was replaced by today's "mean girls," who flex their power by acting like divas. Sisterhood is stronger than that.

Girls like you can revive the idea of sisterhood by spreading respect in your world. You do this when you lead by example, treating other girls like the valuable human beings they are. You show other girls your support by getting to know them before passing judgment and by respecting them—not for what they look like or have, but for who they are on the inside.

6. Fighting for Equality

Though women and girls have made strides, inequality goes on every day. The amount of respect you get can be affected not only by your sex but also by other factors, including age, race, ethnicity, religion, class, sexual identity, or disabilities. Unfortunately, inequality exists. You've probably felt, sensed, or witnessed it at some point in your life.

At the core of respect is a belief that *all* human beings, no matter what their background or way of life, deserve equal treatment. To be treated as an equal, you often have to take action—from fighting for your

INSIDE THE "-ISMS"

These "-isms" have their roots in prejudice. Any time people discriminate against someone based on stereotypes, they're showing prejudice. You've probably heard some of the terms below, but in case you haven't, here's a cheat sheet.

ableism, *n.* Prejudice against people with disabilities.

classism, *n.* Prejudice based on people's social or economic class.

lookism, *n.* Prejudice against people based on their physical appearance.

racism, *n.* Prejudice based on racial background; the belief that one race is superior to another.

sexism, *n.* Prejudice based on gender, usually directed against women and girls.

reTroSPECT: equal rights, THE LONG FIGHT

In 1921, a powerhouse women's rights advocate named Alice Paul wrote the Equal Rights Amendment (ERA) to the U.S. Constitution to legally grant men and women the same rights throughout the country. Seems like a no-brainer matter of respect, right? Still, it wasn't until 1972 that Congress finally adopted a similar amendment that said, "Equality of rights under the law shall not be denied or abridged by the United States or any state on account of sex." But because the amendment was never ratified by the necessary number of states needed to make it the official law of the land, women (and girls) are still not guaranteed full constitutional rights. The National Organization for Women (NOW) and other groups are trying to pass a broader constitutional amendment that would clearly prohibit discrimination based on sex, race, sexual identity, marital status, ethnicity, national origin, color, or indigence (poverty). The fight for equality isn't always easy but it *is* worth the effort, and no girl should ever give up!

rights, to speaking out against injustice, to organizing others to take a stand. You also have to believe that you *are* an equal, in spite of any discrimination you face.

7. Getting Help

Respecting yourself is about learning how to take care of yourself, including knowing when you need help. Making changes in your life or opening other people's eyes to the need for respect can be hard to do alone, especially when you have to stand up to people at school, at work, on the streets, or in your own home. For example, maybe you're being sexually harassed and you know it's wrong but you don't know how to stop it. Or you might have been hurt in the past, and you don't feel like you can sort out all the intense emotions on your own.

In situations like these, it's important to enlist the help of an adult, a trusted friend, a peer counselor, a religious leader, the school counselor, or a professional therapist. You might also need to seek out resources to learn how to take care of yourself, defend yourself, or find supportive environments (such as joining an organization just for girls). Getting help isn't a sign of weakness. When you reach out, it's a sign of strength, and proof that you know you're worth looking out for.

On the road to respect, help is out there. "More Info" starts on page 204 and includes all sorts of resources—from organizations, to books, to helplines you can call if you need support.

Simple Respect Mathematics
Respect myself + Go with my gut + Boundaries! + Speak up
+ Strong relationships + Equality + Helping myself
_____
= RESPECT

The DISH on Disrespect

To understand what respect is, you've also got to know what it's *not*. Here are some examples:

❧ **Using fear and intimidation.** Some people think they can get respect by asserting power over someone else. For example, bullies often use physical harm or public humiliation to scare others. Certain adults might use threats to get you to do something (or to stop doing something). Your peers—and maybe even your friends—might pressure you by saying "Everyone's doing it," and threatening to ruin your reputation if you don't join in. Ruling by intimidation doesn't gain anybody real respect (it just puts people on guard).

❧ **Acting "above" others.** Do you know people who act like they're better than everybody except the exclusive group they hang out with? Or who assume their way of life is the correct one, and that everyone else should do exactly as they do? Or who think they're an authority on everything and hardly listen to a word anyone else says? When people put out this type of attitude, they're being self-righteous (that "It's my way or the highway" or "I'm right, you're wrong" vibe). Respect is about dignity, not acting superior.

❧ **Giving orders.** Do you think showing respect means obeying orders? They're not the same thing at all. If your dad or mom asks you to do something in a polite way, you're more likely to do it because it was a considerate request and you're following the family rules. But if people make demands of you or bark out orders, you probably feel pushed around and insulted. No one likes to be given orders;

GIrLS ON DISrESPECT

A lot of girls feel like people don't acknowledge what we're saying—that no one cares.
—Aisha, 16

Breaking trust, backstabbing, gossiping, putting a friend down in front of others, or not standing up for a friend is totally disrespectful.
—Kayla, 16

Sometimes, when guys don't get what they want from us, they curse girls out or talk about girls in a nasty way.—Alissa, 16

I want guys to look at me like I'm a young lady, not a piece of a--. That means looking into my eyes when I'm talking, and not staring at my chest.—Jasmine, 16

people like to be *asked* in a nice way and to have the opportunity to respond with a yes or a no. That's a natural boundary most of us share.

In general, disrespect happens when someone—including you—violates any of your rights. Disrespect can damage how you see yourself and treat yourself, and the effects can last a long time. You could start to have more family problems, get lower grades, hang out with people who bring you down, or avoid social situations and extracurricular activities—and maybe eventually take harmful risks that hurt your body (and feelings). The result? You might not reach your potential, and that's a really big deal. The world suffers each time a girl doesn't reach her potential. When you're disrespected, the whole world can take a hit because you are *that* important.

To understand how disrespect affects you, take a look at the following scenarios and see if you can relate:

Your right: To feel like you belong and are an equal.

Your right disrespected: When people you care about treat you like you're in the way or a nuisance. When you're excluded. When people look down on you, act like you don't count, or discriminate against you.

How it can feel: Like you don't matter.

Your right: To figure out what you need and take care of yourself.

Your right disrespected: When you do what your friends tell you to do, instead of listening to your gut. When you're hungry but don't eat because you think you have to look like the celebrities you see on TV. When your family piles too many responsibilities on top of all your homework, but you don't think you can ask for help.

How it can feel: Like your body, mind, and heart are breaking down.

Your right: To listen to your true feelings.

Your right disrespected: When you put your feelings, ideas, or needs aside to please others. When you can't trust yourself to do what's right for you. When you ignore your boundaries.

How it can feel: Like you're not being honest with yourself and others.

Your right: To speak your mind, change your mind, and question the world around you.

Your right disrespected: When you're told to be quiet because someone doesn't share your point of view (POV). When you speak up in class, and people roll their eyes or snicker. When you're pressured to do something after you've said no because you've said yes in the past. When someone discourages you from pursuing your interests or questioning the way things are.

How it can feel: Like your opinions, feelings, and boundaries aren't important.

Your right: To be different from your family, your friends, and media ideals and images.

Your right disrespected: When you're treated like you're a disappointment because you're not living up to your family's expectations. When you're pressured to follow the crowd, even when the crowd is making bad choices. When you're harassed because of your beliefs, lifestyle, or background. When you bash your own body or looks, and try to live up to unrealistic images in magazines or on TV.

How it can feel: Like you can't be different or can't be the true you.

Your right: To feel and be safe.

Your right disrespected: When the school hallways are ruled by bullies, cliques, or gossipers. When you're followed or leered at on the streets or in stores. When your home feels dangerous because of how people are treated. When you're emotionally or physically abused in any way.

How it can feel: Like you're always afraid and can't protect yourself.

YOUR RIGHTS

Your right: To become independent.

Your right disrespected: When your family doesn't give you room to grow. When a boyfriend/girlfriend acts jealous of your every move. When your friends try to prevent you from hanging out with anyone else. When you feel like you're being held back in some way at school. When you can't spend time doing activities that you love and that build your self-worth.

How it can feel: Like you can't stretch or reach new heights.

Your right: To follow your passions and be the real you.

Your right disrespected: When you don't allow yourself to try new things because you're afraid you'll look silly or fail. When a friend tells you your hobbies or interests are weird, stupid, or (fill in the blank). When people say your goals are unrealistic or out of your reach. When you cave in to pressure to conform—to be just like everyone else.

How it can feel: Like you can't be yourself or find your true purpose.

Knowing your rights is the first step toward making them a reality. Even if you've been stung by disrespect in the past, you can reclaim your rights and keep moving ahead on the path to respect.

You GET What You GIVE

If you want respect, just use your senses—including common sense—and follow these do's and don'ts.

Seeing. To avoid a case of the "-isms," (page 9), try not to judge others based on the outside instead of getting to know what's inside.

✧ **DO** get to know people before you draw conclusions about their lifestyle, personality, or beliefs.

✤ **DO** notice if you seem to automatically trust certain kinds of people or dislike others based on first impressions.

✤ **Don't** make assumptions about people based on how they look or are dressed (like they're lazy or successful, rich or poor, smart or not so smart, stuck up or sweet). Appearances can be deceiving.

✤ **Don't** show interest only in people who look and act like you. Diversity is the spice of life and getting to know all kinds of people can make your life way more interesting.

Listening. When people make an effort to really listen to each other, it's a major sign of respect. If you use the tips below, you'll probably be surprised at how well people respond.

✤ **DO** make eye contact, which shows you're paying attention. If looking into people's eyes makes you uncomfortable, here's a trick: Look at the middle of their forehead instead (it will appear that you're making eye contact).

✤ **DO** be open to what's being said and avoid passing judgment too quickly.

✤ **DO** nod your head at times during the conversation, which is body language for "I'm listening."

✤ **Don't** cut in with a lot of advice, no matter how much you think the person needs it. Sometimes, people just want to vent and aren't looking for someone to solve their problems for them.

✤ **Don't** tune out of conversations to think about what you want to say next or keep interrupting with your own point of view. Each person needs a chance to talk and be heard.

Speaking. Chances are, at least once in your life you've had disrespectful words slung at you. And they sure can leave a dent in your self-respect. Words carry a lot more weight than you may think. To get into the respect habit, remember to watch what you say and *how* you say it.

❖ **DO** speak to others the same way you want to be spoken to. Make sure your words are considerate and respectful.

❖ **DO** notice the effect of your words. Teasing, offensive jokes, or swearing may not always *seem* like a huge deal, but to some people they are.

❖ **DO** give other people the chance to talk about themselves. Ask them questions to show you're interested.

❖ **Don't** avoid telling people how you feel if they've hurt you or crossed a boundary.

❖ **Don't** sink down to a lower level just to fit into the conversation. If people are gossiping or spreading rumors, you always have the choice to set a boundary or walk away.

❖ **Don't** go off on people. Taking out your frustrations on someone else or yelling to get your point across is disrespectful.

When in doubt, always follow the golden rule: Treat others the way *you* want to be treated.

How Do You Define Respect?

Journaling is a really great way to get to know the real you, or to take notes as you figure out what respect means to you. You can journal in a notebook, in a sketchbook, or on a computer. The cool thing about journaling is that you get to blurt out whatever's in your heart and mind without censoring yourself. To start your own journal about respect and the life, times, and thoughts of Ms. You, try these warm-up questions.

1. What does respect mean to you? What do you think it means to your family and friends?

2. In your life right now, what are some ways you're getting and giving respect? (Think about "The 7 Respect Basics.")

3. Name the people in your life you most respect. Why do you admire them or feel they deserve your respect? (They can be people you know or people you've read about.)

4. Are all of your rights being honored by you and those around you? If so, how? If not, why?

5. Think about some disrespectful situations you've dealt with recently. How did you handle things? What could you have done differently? What might happen next time?

Tip: If people at home don't respect your privacy, find a good hiding place for your journal.

How to Respect Yourself

When Jamila, 16, walks into the crowded teen center at her local library, others seem to take notice. What catches their eye may be the traditional *hijab* (Muslim head-covering) that she wears with pride, but there's something else about her that commands attention. When she starts talking, she's passionate and articulate about education, community service, politics, the future, and her belief that girls can be a powerful force in the world. Jamila also knows her values, and she sticks by them while trying to understand people who are different from her. Mostly, she doesn't hide who she is or what she wants—she celebrates her individuality. She has something special, and she knows exactly what it is: self-respect.

On respect:

"When I want respect, it starts with me first. I have to be sure of who I am. I have to believe in myself. I have to know I have a place in the world—that I do belong. I have to own my emotions and how I feel about something. I have to live with my choices. I think one of the most important things for a girl to remember is that when you don't respect yourself, others won't either."

On the way she lives:

"Having self-respect is about knowing what you like, doing things for yourself, and knowing where you stand. I'm very interested in politics and love to read and dance, so I spend as much time as possible doing that stuff. I do independent study, working with teachers and tutors at my own pace, because taking charge of my education has shown me what I can accomplish. To challenge myself, I also go to special workshops at local universities. To meet other girls and feel like I'm making a difference, I help run meetings for a girl activism organization and help plan a yearly convention for more than a thousand girls."

On feelings and making choices:

"I really try to open my eyes and question myself: *Do I feel OK with that? If no one else was doing that, would I be doing it? Would I still like it?* I always try to figure out my perspective and what I want, so I don't just conform to what others are doing. Being like everyone else is not important to me. When you decide to be yourself, you are more happy and fulfilled."

2

Your Mind

It's safe to say you're going through big—maybe even huge—changes right now. All at once, everything from your relationships, to your thoughts, to your body is changing shape and vying for your attention. You're probably also dealing with countless new feelings or trying to sort out old ones. No matter where you're at, an unstoppable and exciting process has begun: You're becoming more independent and making up your mind about who you want to be.

That's why respect starts on the *inside*. You build it by exploring your beliefs, interests, and feelings so you can make choices that reflect how much you care about yourself. Sound like a lot of work? It is. You have to make an effort every day, but it's worth it. With respect on the inside, you'll have the foundation you need to build respect in other aspects of your life—from taking care of your body, to having strong relationships, to fighting for your rights. Put it this way: Respect is a powerful state of mind.

KNOW That You're Worth It

Having self-respect ultimately means thinking highly of yourself. Not because you're stuck up but because, deep down, you appreciate yourself and want to look out for your interests. And yet, you've probably noticed that people or ideas you come in contact with every day can eat away at you. A friend may make a rude comment

about you. A blockbuster movie might make you want to be skinnier, richer, or more popular. True, these outside forces can leave you feeling like you're not good enough—if you let them. Only *you* determine what you absorb, and how you think about and deal with it.

Imagine your self-worth as a piggy bank: If it's empty or running low, you'll be too broke to pay your respects to yourself and others. To make frequent deposits into your account, try the following ideas and commit to making the investment in *you*.

Admire yourself. Break out your old baby pictures, if you have some, and take a good hard look. The day you were born, you were more valuable than all the cash in the world. While you're staring at mini-you, think about what a miracle you are. That girl in the snapshot is the same girl you're looking at today. You're taller and wiser now—but still as fabulous and valuable. That's the truth.

> Loving yourself is getting up every morning, looking in the mirror, smiling, and knowing you're going to have a great day. It's feeling good about your body, soul, mind, and everything. No one is perfect, and getting through struggles depends on being strong and having faith in yourself. If you can do that, then you're set.
> —Brandy, 16

> I like the way I am unique, smart, loving to my friends and family, beautiful, and original. I love myself because I am exactly who I want to be and choose to be.
> —Alessandra, 15

Find supporters. When you have a desire to mean something to the world—or someone close to you—you're looking for validation. Every girl needs it. Even if you're confident, it still helps to have the support of at least one other person who wants to see you succeed. You can find your own cheering section by hanging out with people who let you know that you matter, tell you what a great job you're doing, or share how inspired they are by you. But the most important thing is validating yourself by thinking and saying, "I count."

Dig deep. At times when you feel low, dig down to the source of those feelings. By digging, we mean just that: You get out the "shovel" and start to dig down to the truth. For example, do you have financial hardships or are you dealing with stereotypes (such as one of the "-isms" on page 9) that make you feel less valuable than other people? Does a family member criticize you a lot, making you doubt yourself? Write about who or what has knocked down your self-worth. Then list the reasons why you *do* deserve to feel good about yourself. The list can be a reminder of what you know in your heart—that you *are* worth it (and then some).

The Real You

Write what's special about yourself and keep the list handy for those times when you're tempted to believe a hurtful comment.

I am unique because: _____

My secret talents are: _____

I feel best about myself when: _____

The things I like most about myself are: _____

I'm worth respecting because: _____

Get to KNOW Yourself Better

Even when you believe in being your own person, you still might feel pressured to fit in. And what does fitting in require? Many girls say they face pressures ranging from having to dress a certain way, to partying like they're ID-carrying adults, to getting sexual or just looking sexual.

In the popular book *Reviving Ophelia: Saving the Selves of Adolescent Girls,* Mary Pipher says that, to fit in, many girls will split into two people: a false self (the one they show the world) and a true self (hidden inside). And groundbreaking feminist writer Simone de Beauvoir argued in her classic book, *The Second Sex,* that teen girls are forced by societal pressures to become "female impersonators" who start aiming to please others instead of themselves because of gender stereotypes. (Like the idea that girls have to take care of others or should have less freedom to be risk takers and leaders than boys.) Well, she still has a point, even though her book was published in 1949.

To be accepted, you might give up the passions and quirks that make the true you shine. Or hide away your true self and pose, act, and try to look like the kind of girl you *think* you should be, or who everyone seems to want you to be. A study by Girls Inc. found that 60 percent of girls believe they experience stereotypes that limit their rights to be themselves, like all females are "feminine," "emotional," "sensitive," or "sexy."[1] That's a lot of girls whose rights aren't being respected—mainly to feel like an equal, to be different, and to be real.

You don't have to make fitting in with the crowd your number one goal, or make choices just to be popular. Being your true self can be lonely at times, but it feels worse to be someone you don't even know (or wouldn't want to know). When you're being real, it can feel like the best thing in the world—because you're living a life that's true to *you*. To keep it real:

Know what you stand for. Every girl develops a code of beliefs that guides her choices in life. Yours might be based mainly on your family's values, your religious upbringing, your cultural background, or your education. Your values are also influenced by your emotions and reactions to events happening in the world. Of course, your friends and other people have an influence, too. Take another look at your code. Are your beliefs truly *yours?* If not, do some soul-searching. Question the world and rules around you. Explore topics that interest or concern you. Have open and thoughtful discussions with your family and friends. Work on developing a code that's right for you.

My Code

In your journal, fill in these statements to figure out what you stand for.

I live by the following beliefs: _____

These beliefs come from: _____

I want to be the kind of person who: _____

I want my life to be: _____

I think all people should treat their fellow human beings like: _____

Discover your passions. Doing activities you enjoy helps you get to know yourself and build confidence. Spend as much time as possible doing activities that make you feel good in ways that are healthy. Have fun fine-tuning your skills, whether they're in sports, music, academics, or the arts. Pursue and conquer challenges like learning a new language or rock climbing—whatever you're curious or excited to learn. If there's one golden asset you can put to work every day to show how much you respect yourself, it's your time.

Pencil Yourself In

Keeping a detailed log of what you do with your time can reveal whether you're distracted from your passions. For one week, try this activity in your journal. (Note: You'll need to keep your journal with you at all times.)

1. Make a passions list. Write down 10–20 things you love to do and why. If you can't think of anything you love to do, write down any activities you sort of enjoy or have always wanted to try.

2. Every day for a week, log your daily activities. Whenever you change activities, write down exactly what you had been doing and for how long. (Example: "8:15 P.M. to 9:30 P.M.: Talked on the phone.")

3. At the end of the week, compare your passions list to your log. Circle all the instances where you spent time doing things from your passions list.

4. Next, look at your log and circle the responsibilities you can't skip, such as going to school or having meals with your family (these might also be passions).

5. Underline the activities you don't really enjoy or that distract you from your true interests. Think about whether you can start eliminating some of these activities from your life.

6. Make an ideal schedule for how you'd spend your week doing all the things you love to do. How might you make this dream a reality? Go over the schedule with an adult who cares about you and ask for help in making your schedule fit your passions.

Set some goals. Suppose you're interested in a particular subject or activity—come up with a plan to explore it. You might talk to experts in that field, apply for an internship, take a volunteer position, and more. By setting goals to pursue your passions, you can quickly learn that you love something more than you thought or, to your surprise, that you aren't that interested in it after all. Accomplishing goals makes you feel proud, which increases your self-respect and confidence.

Road Trip

Have you ever been on a road trip (or dreamed of going on one)? On road trips, most people use maps to get from one place to another. Accomplishing goals is kind of the same idea: going from Point A to Point B, with a bunch of steps in between. Next time you want to tackle a goal, approach it like a road trip and create the map you'll need to get to your destination.

1. On paper, mark where you'll start (Point A) and write your goal in specific words like, "I want to volunteer at the animal shelter two Saturdays per month." An unclear goal like, "I want to do something with animals" is more difficult to reach. Why do you want to accomplish this goal?

2. Draw a line down to the bottom of the page and write Point B (your destination). Then figure out your first step. For example, "First, call the animal shelter for a tour and info on volunteer opportunities." Give yourself a deadline.

3. Next, think about all the other steps to your goal. Consider your time, financial resources, what research you may need to do, and who can help and support you. Set a deadline for when you plan to reach each new step, but be flexible because unexpected roadblocks may throw you off track for a few days or weeks.

4. Once you've actually reached Point B, celebrate. The next time you set a goal, try this again to plot your way from start to finish.

Kick out the party crashers. As you pursue your dreams and goals, you might find that some people don't like the fact that you're doing something great for yourself. They'll tell you why it won't work, or they'll say you'll never be able to do it. Choose to tune out your party crashers by setting a boundary. Say, "That might be your opinion, but I plan to see this goal through.

If you can't support me, I'll talk about it with someone else." Never turn down the volume on your dreams and goals, or conform to someone else's idea of what's good for you.

TUNE IN to Your Feelings and Needs

Emotions are so powerful that sometimes they wash over you and leave you feeling completely out of control. They can make you go through a box of tissues in ten seconds flat (it seems that way at least!), or say and do things you regret. To build your self-respect, keep in touch with your feelings and needs on a daily basis, as if you were calling or IMing your brain and heart. If a person or situation doesn't feel right, makes you uncomfortable, or really offends you, listen to what you're thinking and feeling. You can tune in to your emotions by trying the following tips.

Trust your gut. When you're faced with making a decision, your gut sends you clues about what to do: Is your stomach in knots? Is your heart pounding? If your gut gives you a warning sign or tells you what feels right, pay attention to it. Walk yourself through the different decisions you might make: What do you want to happen? What do you think *will* happen? Which decision makes your gut reaction subside, leaving you calmer and more sure of yourself?

Stick up for yourself. One way you show yourself (and others) that you're worth respecting is by sticking up for yourself. Start by saying how you feel, because no one can argue with that. For example, "When you don't look at me when I'm talking to you, I feel like you're not listening. I need to feel like you're paying attention." Telling people your needs and boundaries can make you nervous, especially if you're new at it. Always check your gut to make sure you feel safe. Tip: Don't start speaking up to the most difficult person you know. Instead, practice setting boundaries with someone you feel comfortable with and who's likely to take you seriously.

Let your feelings out. If you bottle up your feelings, they could spill out in ways that harm your health, your ability to make choices, and other people (like if you blow up at someone in anger or can't have fun with your friends because you're agonizing inside). Let your feelings out! Of course, there's a time and place for everything, and you may not want to get

Bound-a-ries, Please

If you feel like someone's trying to censor your emotions, try saying, "I'm really upset and need a few minutes to myself. I hope you understand," or "Can you hang out with me and not say anything for a few minutes? I don't really want advice right now. Just having you here is helping."

too emotional or do any heavy crying at school, where everyone can see. Go someplace more private, where you can think or write in your journal. Ask your family and friends for their support.

Know you're not alone. Some of the most intense feelings that teen girls experience are frustration, insecurity, anger, and disappointment. At times, these feelings can be overwhelming. If you find yourself stuck reliving difficult emotions over and over to the point where you feel out of control or can't move on, you'll need to take a step back and try to discover their true source. Talk to your friends, adults you trust, or the school counselor for help. For a list of helplines to call, see pages 204–205.

Emotions Takin' Me Over

Respect yourself by exploring where your feelings are coming from and what you can do to work through them. At times when you're feeling strong emotions, you can:

1. Stop whatever you're doing and sit down. If you're right in the middle of a conversation, excuse yourself and take a break.

2. Pay attention to your breathing and name the emotions you're experiencing (sadness, embarrassment, anxiety).

3. In your journal or in your mind, describe how you feel and why. Ask yourself what may have brought up the feelings (choices you've made, old habits that are hard to break, needs that are being neglected).

4. Think about what you'd like to change or have happen. Do you need to take action? How? Who can you talk to for ideas and support? And what can you do to help yourself?

Talk to Yourself with RESPECT

Sometimes, girls can be their own harshest critics. Maybe you walk around with thoughts like, "Everyone's looking at me weird," or "People hate me," when that's not the case at all. Maybe you tell yourself you're not good enough or that you wish you were somebody else. Think about your inner voice: How do you talk to yourself in your head? Are you considerate and kind, constantly critical, or a bit of both? Most of us won't let other people verbally abuse us past a certain point, but when it comes to how we talk to *ourselves*, we hardly set any boundaries at all. You deserve better—here's how to get it:

Be your own best friend. Best friends are the people you can count on and would do almost anything for. Most of us treat our best friends with a lot of respect. (They probably wouldn't be our best friends if we didn't.) Think about how you talk to your best friend: Do you listen to her without judging her? Do you help her pick herself up and brush herself off when she's had a big disappointment? List a few ways that you speak to your best friend with respect and care. Make a point of talking to yourself that way, too. At times when you don't, ask yourself, "Would I talk to my best friend like that?"

Keep your promises to yourself. You know what happens if someone promises you something and then goes back on that promise: You feel betrayed and hurt. The same thing happens when you make a promise to yourself that you don't keep. The more empty promises you make, the more let down you feel. Suppose you promise yourself again and again that you're going to start getting better grades, and then you blow off your homework the next day and give up. Ask yourself what's going on: Do you need to set more specific and reachable goals? Do you need help? Are old habits getting in the way of true change? Do you really *want* to do what you keep promising yourself you'll do, or is it something you think you *should* do because someone else told you it was a good idea? Honoring your promises to yourself starts with being honest when you make them.

Filter criticism. If someone makes a rude comment about you, dishes out a criticism, or says something honest (maybe too honest) that was meant to be "helpful" but came out all wrong, how do you react? Do you immediately take it to heart, believing what the person said or letting it plant a seed of self-doubt? It's not easy to ignore critical remarks, but it's definitely possible. This is where "filter boundaries" come in. Ask yourself if there's any truth to what the person said, and be honest with yourself about it. If there's not any truth to it, then ignore the criticism and remind yourself it's not about *you*. Think, "Well, that's obviously something she has an issue with—it's not my problem." But if there *is* some truth to what the person said, decide if there's anything you can do to make a positive change for yourself. For example, you might think, "Yeah, it's true I'm a little flaky at times. I could be better at calling people back."

Instant Replay

Negative thoughts can play in your head like a broken record. But there *is* a way to change your tune and stop playing the "Bash Yourself Blues."

1. Write down a list of harsh things you say to yourself or rude comments that you can't get out of your mind.

2. The next time you catch yourself replaying the comments, stop. Tell yourself, "I'm not going to talk to myself that way."

3. Then rewind by going back and replacing the negative thoughts with positive ones about yourself like, "My family loves me," or "I scored a goal in soccer last week, and the whole team cheered for me." You could also re-record something simple like, "I believe in myself," or "I deserve respect." The positive thoughts will energize you and help you feel more optimistic again.

4. Replay them until you feel better or any time you start bashing yourself again.

Have Confidence and Courage

Any self-respecting choice requires confidence and courage (C&C). It takes courage to choose to speak up and let someone know how you feel, especially if that person has authority over you (like a teacher or parent). It takes confidence to try new things. It takes courage *and* confidence to put yourself first. The good news is that any girl can work on pumping up her C&C.

Recognize your C&C. Confidence is that "I can do it" feeling. Chances are, you've felt it at some point. Maybe it was right before a game, when you knew you had the edge over the competition. Maybe it was before a test, when you'd studied hard and knew your stuff. It's that feeling of "I'm ready, bring it on!" Courage, on the other hand, isn't necessarily the *absence* of fear. Sometimes, courage is about being scared and going ahead with something anyway. Think about a time when you did this yourself—how did it feel?

> I don't try to impress people with qualities that aren't mine or pretend to be someone I'm not. I just show off who I am, because I believe that people should accept me for who I am.
> —Alexia, 14

Start small. To build your C&C, take small risks where you have a good chance of succeeding (like when you already know you can do two out of the three steps required). For example, if you need an after-school job, go for the job where you already meet a few of the qualifications so you're more likely to be hired. Maybe you babysit your younger siblings and know how to lead them in playing games, so you feel confident about applying for your first job at the library reading to small children. By accomplishing this step first, you can gain more skills to go after a more challenging goal, like becoming a reading tutor. After you gain confidence by conquering small risks, you'll feel ready to take bigger ones. Each new challenge can build your confidence even more.

Face fears. Have you ever avoided trying something new because you were afraid? Fear can be your gut's way of warning you, though *too many* fears can hold you back from taking a risk or going after a dream. Are you afraid of failing (so you avoid advanced classes at school)? Looking silly in front of others (so you won't go out for the dance team)? Or that if things don't work out, you'll never get another chance (so you skip entering big contests or competitions)? To overcome fears like these, think about their source. Often, fears come from being uncomfortable with the unknown or feeling out of control. But sometimes, the cause is that you don't believe you deserve success. Boost yourself up by telling yourself that you

Gut Check

Fear that makes your stomach jump a little is different from a gut feeling that something's wrong or dangerous. If you're in physical danger—like a stranger's following you—trust your gut. But if you're not in physical danger, question where your fear is coming from and then decide if you need some C&C to face the challenge. With practice, you can begin to tell the difference between your instincts and fears.

can do it and *are* worth it. To calm your mind and body, try some deep breathing or take a long walk.

Be imperfect. Lots of girls are on the "be-perfect treadmill," believing they have to look and be perfect in order to be accepted and loved. You don't need to do everything right or be number one all the time. To build confidence, skip trying to be perfect and live on the edge a little. Practice taking risks where you're sure to make some mistakes (like if you love to sing but think you sound awful, take singing lessons or join a choir). When it comes to any activity or goal, try to define and measure up to your own yardstick—your personal best.

SISTERHOOD

One way to build sisterhood is by telling other girls and women how much you admire them. If your heroine isn't someone you come into contact with day to day and is a living person, you can let her know how you feel about her by writing her a letter. (You can ask a librarian for help in finding the person's contact information, if needed.) Describe any common interests you share, how she inspires you, or how you'd like to be like her. The letter can be a confidence booster for both of you, and you could even end up with a great mentor.

Find heroines. Having heroines comes in really handy when you're building up your C&C. Your heroine or role model (and you can have more than one) could be someone in your family, in your community, or in the public eye. She might even be someone from the past—a historical or religious figure, for example. She could be a politician, an athlete, an artist, a performer, or a newsmaker. She might even be fictional—a literary character, a TV persona, or a mythological figure. No matter who she is, she needs to have meaning to you and traits that inspire you to reach for your own dreams and goals. What do you admire about your heroine? What qualities of hers do you aspire to have? You can read the biographies of heroines or explore their lives through movies and the Internet.

Show your stuff. When you let yourself shine, your self-respect grows and you feel great about who you are. But do you find it difficult to show your star power and sing your own praises to others? Girls don't always learn to pump themselves up the ways guys do, because girls are often taught to be

I like who I am because I think everyone is special and unique in their own way. Every girl has at least one reason to be happy with herself—take that good thing and focus on it.
—Amanda, 14

modest about their accomplishments. This is a gender stereotype that every girl has to battle. You can start showing your stuff by recognizing it within yourself and by telling others about the talents you bring to a situation. To build your C&C, constantly remind yourself, in your head or on paper, of your accomplishments and abilities. Then take action. For example, you might lobby to get the slot as yearbook editor or convince the softball coach to play you in a new position. When you have something special to offer or have proven that you should be given a chance, speak up and show up!

LEARN from Mistakes

Making your own choices is part of becoming a bona fide woman, yet sometimes you'll do things that you wish you could tweak or take back. (Like you didn't trust your gut, didn't stick with a boundary, or didn't speak up when you knew you should have.) Sometimes, part of learning who you are—and what you'd never do again even if someone offered you a million dollars—starts with a little leap before you think about the consequences. Even when you're confused, a voice inside you might say, "Are you *sure* you want to do that?" When you hear that alarm, listen to it.

But no matter how hard you try to make the best choices and go for your goals, there will be times when things don't work out. Don't let past disappointments haunt you or become so afraid of failure that you can't move forward. Mistakes are part of life. Try to learn from them while learning about yourself.

Don't let a mistake define you. Every single girl or woman has made a choice or decision she regrets. (And some of us have made a lot of them!) You've probably had a few warnings about Big Stupid Mistakes from parents, teachers, and other adults. They tell you that making bad choices can ruin your life or go on your permanent record. Are they right? Sometimes. Some mistakes can have long-lasting effects—and the adults in your life know this because they've seen people get hurt (and they don't want this to happen to you). But your mistakes are not *you*. Mistakes are learning experiences, not character traits, no matter how painful the lesson.

Look for the lesson. If you make a mistake or don't do something just the way you'd planned, analyze what happened and what you'd do differently next time. Instead of punishing yourself with talk like, "I'm so stupid," or "I always mess everything up," ask yourself, "What did I learn here?" To keep your self-respect intact, don't kick yourself when you're down: Find the lesson. That's the part you don't want to forget.

Stay strong. When a door is slammed in your face (like you worked up the courage to run for student government and didn't win), it's hard not to feel rejected. You've probably heard this before: Life is full of disappointments. And it's totally true. How you handle them has a lot to do with your self-respect. You can let a setback knock you flat and never try again. Or you can choose to grow stronger after a disappointment by bouncing back.

Forgive. If you need to apologize to someone (including yourself) after you've made a mistake, don't delay and don't make excuses. Once you forgive, you can make better choices and continue to care about yourself—without lugging around guilt that can weigh you down.

Bouncing Back

It happens: a bad decision, a mistake, a setback. Now what? Connecting the dots can help you see what went wrong and why—and give you a path for moving forward.

What happened? At the top of a piece of paper, write about the event you're concerned about. Circle it.

How were you feeling? Draw a line from the event and write about the emotions that led up to it. Did you feel insecure, nervous, excited, confused?

What motivated you? Draw a line connecting your feelings to their source. What did you need or want at the time?

Has this happened before? Draw a line from your motives and write about any instances when something similar occurred, if you can remember.

What next? Make the final connecting line by thinking about whether your motives were good or bad at the time. Was anyone hurt by your actions (besides yourself)? Do you need to apologize and forgive? What might you do differently next time? Are you a stronger person from this experience? Why or why not?

Make CHANGES

Getting to know yourself and getting over mistakes sometimes means you have to make changes (like deciding to follow your dreams, behaving differently, or trying to break a habit). Most people don't just decide to change and then instantly change. Many experts say it's a process that takes time and requires specific steps to make the change "stick." Here are three steps to try:

1. Get clear on your reasons. After completing "Bouncing Back" or analyzing some past mistakes, you might be inspired to make a change. Think about your reasons for changing and write them in your journal, if this helps you see things more clearly. Why do you need to make this change? How will it affect your self-respect?

2. Come up with a plan. Decide exactly *how* you'll tackle the change. Don't set your expectations too high, like plotting to change in one day. You might find it helpful to use the "Road Trip" steps on page 24, or just write your plan in your journal. Are there any potential roadblocks? How might you deal with them? Who can you count on for help and support?

3. Get going and stay on track. Even if you've planned things carefully, you might discover that you need to make adjustments. Go back to your plan and tweak your steps. But if you've had a big setback (like you've fallen into a habit you were trying to break), it might be time to return to the first step and rethink your whole process. Don't give up—you'll get there eventually! When the change finally sticks, congratulate yourself for making a positive difference in your life. You might even write yourself a note in your journal, saying what the change has meant to you.

The Picture of Self-Respect

What would a self-portrait of your respect on the inside look like? Take these steps to get a picture of your respect state of mind:

1. Draw a picture or make a collage of yourself. Around it, draw symbols or write words that show how you treat yourself.

2. List any ideas you have for improving your self-respect. You can use the exercises throughout the chapter to build the self-respect you totally deserve.

3. Create a picture or collage of yourself afterward. What does this new "outside" say about how you feel on the inside?

MY BODY, MYSELF

When we asked girls about how they treat their bodies, their answers proved that body respect is about more than what meets the eye: **It starts on the inside.**

I used to diet to lose weight, but then I got so spacey that I couldn't think or do my schoolwork. You need to figure out how to take care of yourself so that you can accomplish what you want to do.—Lisa, 18

When it comes to my body, I've learned to sit alone and ask myself how I really feel and if I'm treating myself right.—Selena, 16

I am beautiful because I say I am, not because someone else thinks I am.—Taylor, 15

I don't care what people think about me. I'm just the right size for me.—Brooke, 15

I deserve to be respected for how I think and how I speak, and not to be looked at as a sex object.—Kamilah, 16

I love who I am as a person, and I feel that I deserve to be listened to when it comes to my body.—Sophia, 15

3

Your Body

Have you heard of the mind-body connection? Basically, it means your mind and body are inseparable and work together around the clock. If you pay close attention, you'll notice that every day your mind and body constantly pass notes and whisper to each other about your physical and emotional needs. How you think and feel on the inside affects how you treat your body. And the way you treat your body then sends supportive or hurtful messages to your mind.

In other words, to have true respect on the inside, you have to treat your body right. This means taking care of yourself physically, enforcing your body boundaries, and speaking up about what works for you (or doesn't). When you respect yourself, you show your body how much you care. You treat yourself to fun outings or yummy meals, and support yourself through athletic, artistic, or adventurous goals.

If taking care of your body is so essential, then you might wonder why so many girls treat their body more like their worst enemy than their best friend. Many girls say this happens when they're trying to fit in. To feel accepted, they try to live up to unrealistic body ideals or become someone they're not. As a result, they may neglect their body, ignoring when they're hungry, tired, uncomfortable, or scared. At times, they may go on strict diets, dress in styles that don't fit with who they are, or experiment in ways that go against their boundaries.

For some girls, the pressure to fit in leads to a mind-body disconnect. And no wonder: A close look at the state of the media today reveals that you and your friends are the most sexualized group of girls in history (meaning girls are seen as sex objects, or made more sexual by what they're exposed to). Even if you aren't sexually active and don't want to be, images all around you seem to say that girls should dress and be hot. Isn't it weird how you can read a true story in a magazine about a girl who's doing courageous things to make the world a better place, and then flip the page and see pictures of a young star all dolled up and striking a seductive pose? Not to mention TV shows and movies featuring entire schools full of girls who look like they were created in a Barbie factory.

Even if you reject these images or know they're nothing like real life, all those sexy-girl stereotypes can creep into your brain. Research shows that these images *do* affect how girls see and treat themselves. Trying to fit in, hating your body, and feeling pressure to lure attention with sex appeal can leave you confused about how to treat yourself, or make it difficult to decide what body respect means to you.

Being the true you comes down to seeing your body as more than a billboard to get attention, acceptance, or love from other people. Look at your body in terms of how it will help you serve your purpose in life and meet your goals. Think of it as your permanent residence—your home sweet home. You only have one body to cart around that smart brain of yours, and that's why treating your body with respect is a must.

WHEN GIRLS DIS THEIR BODIES

I've never met a girl who hasn't said at least once, "I'm so fat!" or "If only my boobs were a little bigger."—Abby, 15

I used to drink a lot. I have smoked pot and experimented with some other drugs. I am not proud of it. I can't believe I was so careless with myself.—Latasha, 15

I compare my body to other girls' bodies to see why guys like them better, or just out of jealousy.—Tamara, 15

My older sister thinks she needs to get her nose, arms, and legs done by a plastic surgeon. It hurts me that she doesn't see herself the way I do: perfect the way she is.—Marabel, 14

I find myself being incredibly rude to my body when the romance department isn't doing so well.—Anna, 14

Girls can lie to others through their appearance—like that they're healthy when they're not—but they are lying to themselves as well.—Lacey, 15

REAL Beauty

There's a type of beauty that's more powerful than the physical type: inner beauty. You probably know people who aren't Hollywood beautiful and look nothing like the images of beauty promoted in movies or magazines, but they are incredibly attractive anyway. They seem to radiate with energy and charm. Or maybe you know older women in your life—like grandmothers, great aunts, or your mom—who still glow with wisdom and a beauty all their own. What stands out about these people? You're looking at *real* beauty. It's not skin deep or silicone induced—and it's timeless.

Here's a beauty tip you might not get from any magazine: Every girl who is self-respecting *is* beautiful. Beauty that glows from the inside never fades as long as you're feeling it. Your real beauty sparkles when you have confidence, compassion, curiosity, and love for yourself. It shows in the genuine smile that lights up your face, in the way you carry yourself with strength. It's reflected in your posture when you're walking tall. It can be seen in how you embrace your heritage and the physical traits you were given by your ancestors.

When you show the real you, you *do* look extra fabulous. Because when you respect yourself, you make sure your body is healthy, cared for, and comfortable. Have you ever seen the opposite of real beauty? Like when a girl has nice features but her attitude makes her seem unattractive? When you have respect or disrespect on the inside, you wear it on the outside.

Real beauty isn't just about attitude. It can be expressed in how you accessorize your body, too. If you feel worthy on the inside, then your clothing, hair, and skin will probably reflect that. And not because you're spending major bucks on your bod but because you take good of care it. If you're down because you don't look like a supermodel (which most of us don't), remember that you have your own inner beauty that's totally unique—you just have to give it an opportunity to shine.

FYI: The Surge in Cosmetic Surgery

The number of plastic surgery procedures performed on girls under age 18 was five times higher in 2003 than it was in 1992, according to the American Society of Plastic Surgeons.[1] Nose jobs were the most popular, with breast augmentations and lifts in second place. Experts say that many girls are going under the knife (even getting procedures as gifts from their parents) in an endless quest for outward perfection. These extreme makeovers also have been turned into "reality TV" shows, spreading the myth that "To look good is to feel good." Yet, that's obviously not the case when so many plastic surgery patients keep going back for additional procedures that are painful and often dangerous.

Making Body CHOICES

One of your rights is to figure out what you need and take care of yourself. Yet, a lot of girls find this hard to do because they don't feel in charge of their bodies in the first place. Politicians make laws, or parents make rules, that dictate what you can and can't do with your body. The media sets beauty standards that probably don't match up with your DNA. People pressure you to ingest unhealthy stuff or take physical risks because they're doing it or want to sell you a product. Or, in the worst cases, an abuser has come along and hurt you, and made you feel totally powerless over your body.

No matter what has happened in your life up to this point, your body still belongs 100 percent to you. Which means that your choices about your body have to be totally you, too. Treating your body well is never a part-time job: It's a lifelong pursuit.

Choice: How You Think About Your Body

Your body image is how you see yourself in the mirror, picture yourself in your mind, or talk to yourself about your body. Having a negative body image—that is, seeing yourself inaccurately or bashing your body—is a widespread problem for girls. Case in point: Only 9 percent of high school girls are overweight according to medical standards, but four times that number (36 percent) think they are.[2]

Often, girls base their unrealistic standards and negative body talk on what they see in the media, or on criticism from friends or family members. You learn a lot from your family, so it's no surprise that unhealthy ideas about food, weight, and appearance can be passed down from your mom or dad. However, you can decide to take care of yourself in healthier ways. You always have a right to be different from your family and friends, or the media images you see.

Beating yourself up over body flaws or obsessing over how to change them sends a message to yourself that you're not good enough. If you constantly tell yourself that your body is ugly, then you're more likely to diet or overeat, to lose confidence, and to resist giving your body what it needs. On the other hand, appreciating your body and its functions can nurture your self-respect.

Body confidence shows in how you carry yourself—that is, how you walk, talk, and present yourself to the world. Think about the amazing things your body can do and compliment your unique assets. This type of positive self-talk, like noticing the features that show you're strong and healthy, helps you to make respectful choices about your body.

Choice: How You Look and Dress

Unless you live in a sunny nudist colony, you have to get ready every day to face the world. The way you dress, make up your face, style your hair, or even pierce yourself all can be reflections of who you are or who you're trying to be. Sometimes, though, the statements you make with your appearance aren't about your individuality or reflecting your inner beauty. They're more about media messages and friends telling you which styles are "in," or seeking attention by dressing in a way that gets you looked at.

Ask yourself if your style is all your own, or if it's a result of trying to fit in or stand out to get extra attention. What does your appearance say about the real you? Do you feel comfortable and confident? Your look doesn't have to please anyone else or even be modest to be self-respecting. To the contrary: Your look should be all about your personality and what makes you feel good about yourself. No matter what your style, always think about whether it's truly respectful of your mind and body.

Choice: How You Feed Your Body

You need to eat healthy foods packed with vitamins and minerals to nourish your body and feel great. Some girls truly enjoy food without guilt and know how to make smart food choices. However, other girls start to have a messed-up relationship with food, starving themselves or going on exercise binges because someone called them "chubby," or because they're trying to live up to unrealistic standards. Many teen girls say it's hard for them to make nutritional choices that support their physical and emotional health. For instance, 59 percent of high school girls say they're trying to lose weight, and almost the same number (56 percent) admit they eat less food to do so.[3]

It's no surprise that with rail-thin stars as role models many girls become dissatisfied with themselves and start eating in unhealthy ways. Consider that the average American woman is 5'4" tall and weighs 140 pounds, while the average American model is 5'11" and weighs 117 pounds.[4] In her book *The Beauty Myth: How Images of Beauty Are Used Against Women,* Naomi Wolf reveals that the average actress or model is thinner than 95 percent of the female population (and her book was published in 1991—stars are notably *even skinner* now).[5]

reTroSPECT:
DOeS THe DIeTING TreND WeAKeN YOUr POWer?

In *The Beauty Myth*, author Naomi Wolf uncovers that just after Western women got the right to vote in 1920—which gave them more power and say than ever before—a "great weight shift" began. Basically, Wolf concludes that females became preoccupied with trying to become 10–15 pounds below their normal weight.[7] Extreme dieting ensued and is still here today.

So what's the respect connection? As Wolf writes, the great weight shift deprives females' brains and bodies of the fuel they need to grow, achieve, and, well, take over the world! When we don't eat enough food, we may become "passive, anxious, and emotional," according to Wolf. Although she doesn't pinpoint one culprit for this trend, she does offer some clues, such as how women's media has changed over the years, with the ideal female becoming skinnier and skinnier.

When you're undernourished, you become tired and your mind doesn't work as well. And, in the worst case, you could get sick or die. If you constantly think about how to stay skinny and make yourself weak with restrictive dieting, you're unable to be the true force you were intended to be. Prolonged hunger or binge cycles can affect your grades and/or athletic performance, or make you too worn out to pursue your passions. Ultimately, girls who focus all their energy on dieting could miss out on a lot in life. That's some serious food for thought.

The dangers of a distorted mind-body connection are real. Millions of people in the United States have an eating disorder such as anorexia (starving themselves to lose weight) or bulimia (purging what they eat through forced vomiting or use of laxatives), or a binge-eating disorder such as compulsive overeating.[6] Both extreme dieting and obesity are on the rise among girls and can lead to lasting health problems or, in the most serious cases, an early death.

Think about the choices you make every day about what and how you eat. Eating is natural, and you're entitled to listen to your body's nutritional needs. When we were babies, we had this idea down. We cried when we were hungry, ate what we needed to grow, and stopped when we'd had our fill. Your body still tells you when you're hungry or thirsty, so you have to listen to your gut— your *actual* gut, in this case— to make choices that support a healthy mind and body.

You've got to stay healthy to fulfill your purpose in life (even if you don't know your entire mission yet). You eat well by making sure you have a balanced intake of foods that provide your body with the vitamins, minerals, protein, and fiber it needs to function and grow. To learn more about eating right, you can talk to a healthy adult you trust or see a doctor. Turn to "More Info" for a list of books and Web sites about body and health (pages 207–208).

Choice: How You Move

You have to get moving to energize yourself, stay strong, deal with stress, and keep your feelings in balance. Experts say that daily exercise is necessary for a healthy mind and body. In a study by the Centers for Disease Control, 55 percent of high school girls reported that they do vigorous exercise at least three days a week.[8] Ideally, even more girls should get healthy doses of exercise.

Take a look at the choices you're making about physical activity. Do you get enough? Any at all? Too much? Maybe you stay glued to the couch instead of going for a walk. Or maybe when you exercise you act as if you're training for the Olympics because you're convinced you've got to melt away those curves and look like a stick. When exercise is taken too far— or you don't get enough— you can do serious long-term damage to your body.

The key is to aim for balance by choosing activities you look forward to, so you feel better about your body. When you exercise for your overall health—and not to look like a celebrity or model—that's self-respect. You're also being good to yourself because the chemicals that are released in your body when you exercise can energize you, help you sleep at night, and make you feel better (ever heard of a "runner's high"?). Exercise also clears your mind and lifts you up, even if you don't feel like moving at first. Plus, you get physically stronger, which can help if you have to chase after a bus, compete on the playing field, or use some self-defense moves.

Try to do something every day to strengthen your body. Go to gym class, join a sports team at school or in your community, or take advantage of your family's membership to a health club if they have one. Go on walks, long hikes, or bike rides on the weekend. Go outside when you can: Getting some natural light each day helps you feel better and more energetic, and keeps your sleeping habits regular. Stay focused on treating your body well and being healthy—realistic goals that you can reach for all your life.

Working Out Respect for Your Bod

If exercise is already a part of your life or you know you want it to be, take a look at your habits and see where you might improve.

1. List what you do for daily or weekly exercise, and why you like each activity. Think about what motivates you and how you feel before and after working out.

2. If you don't exercise, try to find out why. List your reasons (or excuses). Think about why you have a hard time with physical activity and how you might change that.

3. If needed, set a goal to get moving (see "Road Trip" on page 24 for tips). Consider teaming up with some friends and exercising together, which is a great way to support each other.

Choice: How You Deal with Drugs, Tobacco, or Alcohol

Sooner or later you might be offered mind- or body-altering substances—75 percent of high school students have given them a try.[9] For many, being a teenager is about experimentation, including deciding whether to try drugs, cigarettes, or alcohol. These choices come with a lot of responsibility and consequences.

You've probably gotten some education about why you should stay away from illegal substances. We know you're the kind of girl who can do the homework and learn about the health risks involved—but there's something else to consider, too. Putting those toxins in your body can lead to a mind-body disconnect. When you're using drugs or alcohol, it's just harder to be healthy, make good decisions, listen to your gut, or set and stick to boundaries. To stay strong (body and mind), you'll need to carefully weigh the risks of substances that could affect your health and self-respect.

If someone offers you something you think could harm your body, try, "No thanks, it's not for me." You can tell the person why—that's totally up to you—but be sure not to sound like you're making excuses. Always be strong and don't laugh when you set a body boundary. Let the person know you're serious. Remember: Your real friends will respect your choices and won't keep pressuring you to go against your body boundaries.

Think Ahead

When it comes to drugs, tobacco, or alcohol, think about your boundaries by completing these thoughts in your journal:

I want to try a certain substance because: _____

I want to avoid certain substances or experiences because: _____

The health/emotional risks are: _____

My values and beliefs about using illegal substances include: _____

If I'm pressured into smoking, drinking, or doing drugs, I will say: _____

Based on my past experiences, I want to set new boundaries/make changes including: _____

Choice: How You Take Physical Risks

We're all for girls exploring who they are, what they stand for, and what they like to do. But in many circumstances you have to decide if your body is safe or at risk. Jumping into iffy situations for the love of spontaneity could put your body on

FYI: Girls and Self-Harm

Some girls purposely harm their bodies, performing self-mutilation, self-injury, or cutting. These girls cut, scar, bruise, or burn themselves, not necessarily because they're suicidal, but to feel a sense of control. They inflict physical pain as a sudden release from bottled-up emotional pain, such as depression or anxiety. In other words, they create physical scars to express their emotional scars. It's estimated that more than 2 million people in the United States self-injure, and cutting is most common among females.[10] Often, girls who self-mutilate also suffer from eating disorders, are perfectionists, or have been physically or sexually abused.

On pages 204–205 of "More Info," you'll find helplines you can call for support. It takes courage to ask for help. Know that you don't have to keep your pain a secret—get some advice from a trusted adult so you can start healing on the inside.

the line if you don't weigh the risks. Be it pulling pranks, sneaking out, or hanging out with people you're just not sure about, you could get into some sticky situations that put your body in harm's way.

At times, you might find yourself in a risky situation where you've got only moments to decide what to do to keep yourself safe and healthy. Remember these questions so you can play them in your head quickly and make the best choice:

- Is it safe? Why or why not?

- What's the worst that could happen, and is it worth it?

- Is there a way to make it less risky?

- Is it something I think I'll really enjoy, or am I being pressured?

You are your body's number one pro-tector. Deep down inside you know what feels right, wrong, or somewhere in be-tween. Trusting your gut is about not giving in to pressure to take risks with your body, or trying things you might later regret.

Develop Your ASSETS

We know that you already get plenty of advice about how to make over your look. Here are some respect-building ways to make over how you treat your body:

Listen to Your Body

Your body gives you messages all day long. When you're physically hurt, you feel pain, right? Or when you're sick, your body practically forces you to sleep. And when you're about to give a speech in class, you get those familiar butterflies. Check in with yourself all the time to see how you're feeling and what your body or brain might need. Are you thirsty? Drink water. Are you tired? Get some rest. Are those platform shoes killing your feet? Ditch 'em. Hungry? Eat a balanced meal or snack. To actually *get* your body's messages, try to pay attention to your physical needs—and then honor them.

Fine-Tune Your Mind-Body Connection

To hone your mind-body connection, you can also try meditating. Meditation lets you hear and feel everything from your breath to the tingling in your toes, and helps you calm down if you're stressed or worried. Mostly, it encourages you to feel what it's like to be fully *inside* your body. Here's how to do it:

- Find a quiet, private place. This could be in a park or a room at home. You can sit up with straight posture, lie down on your back, or even meditate while soaking in the bathtub.

- Close your eyes and breathe deeply, through your nose

How I Got Body Respect

Juliette, 16, has gone through some tough times where she thought the worst about her body, but now she works on accepting herself and supporting her body instead of being hard on it. Taking good care of herself, she says, gives her the strength to do what she loves, like volunteering, working part-time at a childcare center, and studying to get into film school one day. Here's how she learned to put her health and self-respect first.

On body disrespect:

"When I was watching too much TV or when all of my magazines came in the mail, I would suddenly want to do extra workouts, or I'd see my favorite foods and say, 'I'm not going to eat that.' Before my workouts, I used to go to the Britney Spears Web site, pull up a picture of her abs on the computer screen, and maximize it. Then I'd put on her album and do tons of sit-ups until I couldn't move. I was using her image for how I wanted to look. Eventually, I realized that I wasn't accepting myself and that perfect abs can't define me. Plus, there is so much more to me than that!"

On treating her body well:

"I love to be active, but I make sure I enjoy myself. If I've been eating too much junk, I try to get back to a better balance—more for my brain than the size of my butt. I go on hikes with my friends, and we feel really good when we get to our destination—it's so relaxing. When I feel bad about myself, I listen to music for an hour and just rest and think positive thoughts. And though guys can be immature and make comments about my body, I just ignore them or set them straight. I don't get close to guys, even as friends, unless they like me for me. Rude comments aren't gonna win over my heart."

and out of your mouth. Count to five as you breathe in, and backward from five as you breathe out. (So you're sure to breathe deeply and evenly.) Listen to your breathing and try to ignore any other sounds.

- As thoughts come up, let them go by concentrating on your breathing. If they hang around, acknowledge them and then let them go. Return your focus to your breathing.

- Once you feel you've meditated for around 10 minutes without being distracted, you can stop. Try to work up to 20 or 30 minutes of meditation each time.

Enjoy What Your Body Can Do

You have talents you already know about and others you have yet to discover, and some of these are physical talents. So while you're exploring your personal style, take time to find your thing when it comes to physical activity. Research shows that girls who participate in sports—even for fun, not competitively—have more self-respect and higher confidence, go to college in greater numbers, and are less likely to abuse alcohol or drugs, or have sex before they're ready.

To really stir things up, try a physical activity you thought seemed out of your league in the past (ever want to try yoga, football, or horseback riding?). Or try out for a new sport at school. If you need inspiration, try combining the activity with a health-related cause (like shaking the night away at a dance-a-thon to support an organization you care about). If you're physically disabled or a wheelchair user, join a club that plans outings and sporting events that meet your needs, or read publications that promote respect for your body.

Record Your Body Thoughts

Even if you don't spend tons of time worrying about your appearance, how much is too much? When you're overly focused on your looks, you may neglect other activities, including learning about the world and yourself. And that limits you from becoming everything you could be. Take note of your body thoughts:

Start a log. For one week, add up the time you spend each day obsessing about your body, weight, features, or skin. How do you feel when you're thinking about yourself in a negative way? The following week, spend that exact same amount of time doing something for someone else, exploring an activity you're interested in, meditating, and resting when you need to. Compare the two different weeks. How did you feel when focusing on something other than your appearance?

Keep track of your own "lookisms." How do you see others on the outside? Do you notice their looks, race, physical abilities, weight, style, or clothing? Do you take time to get to know other girls before you size them up? What kind of respect do you show others based on their appearance?

Create a body rights list. How do you want to treat your body? How do you want others to treat it? Make a list of your personal body rights and how you'll honor them.

Get to Know Your Body

Do you know where you came from? We're not talking about the birds and the bees—we're talking about your family history. Learning more about your own family genes can help you understand the real reasons why the other kind of jeans fit you the way they do. You are who you are, thanks to basic anatomy and family genes.

Look at family pictures. Why is your hair that color? Why are your feet that size? Check out photos of family members, relatives, and ancestors to see who you most resemble. Noticing the features that have been handed down to you can help you appreciate yourself—just the way you were born—and take pride in your roots.

Talk to a doctor. To be in the know about your body, you need to learn some basics about how girls' bodies develop and get involved in your medical care. For example, do you need to start getting an annual Pap test (an exam that involves keeping tabs on your reproductive system)? Are you at risk for any health issues as a result of your family's medical history or your cultural background? How much exercise and sleep do you require? Are you making healthy food choices? What else do you need to know?

Pay attention in health class. Most schools offer a health class that explains how your body works and the ins and outs of puberty (all those amazing changes you're experiencing or have gone through already). So take notes and ask questions. If you're not learning this stuff in school, now is the time to do some extra credit. Ask a parent, the school nurse, or a librarian to recommend some resources on girls' health. They're sure to be page-turners, and you'll learn how you tick and how to take the best care of your body.

SISTERHOOD

To pump up other girls' successes or self-image, stop yourself from telling your friends, "You look so skinny!" Try, "I like the way you explained your ideas to _____ and how she really seemed to listen to you." Focus on what your friends do, how they treat others, or what makes them special. When you recognize qualities other than looks, you'll start to compliment yourself that way, too. Remember, there's more to people (including you) than what's on the outside.

Be a Body Role Model

Are you tired of girls being complimented only for their appearance, instead of what's inside? If we only praise each other for our exterior packaging, how can we expect the rest of the world to give our minds and talents the respect and consideration they deserve?

Research shows that girls have a better chance of improving their body image and how they treat their body when they're advocates for younger girls. And younger girls need the encouragement: 51 percent of 9- and 10-year-olds say they feel better about themselves if they diet.[11] Next time you want to give your friends, your little sister, or girls in your neighborhood a compliment, skip commenting on their appearance. Give girls credit for their individuality, creativity, interests, and goals.

Mix Up Your Female Ideals

Body role models can lead you to dig or dis yourself nonstop. If your body idols are too perfect or look nothing like the real girls and women you know, your body standards could get totally out of whack.

Instead of looking at the usual suspects for body ideals—celebs in magazines, on TV, or in movies—try to notice all kinds of female body types. Find reality models: While you're on the bus, in stores, or around your neighborhood, take a closer look at the huge variety of women and girls. Don't pass judgment on them or compare yourself to them—instead find what's unique about each one. Isn't it amazing how every single girl and woman is different? Notice more than surface characteristics, like skin or hair. How does each woman carry her body? Who seems really confident and who seems less so—and why? Find body role models who provide healthy inspiration and, most of all, work on making your unique beauty your real ideal.

Celebrate Your Body Benefits

Every body part has a purpose that has nothing to do with how it looks. Athletes, dancers, and on-the-go girls know all about this. Your body helps make it possible for you to do your favorite activities and to live your life, for that matter. Being aware of your body's unique assets and abilities will help you build a stronger sense of self-respect. And that's what makes you truly beautiful and strong, inside and out.

What My Body Does for Me

Make a list of your body parts, from head to toe. For each part, write something meaningful that it does for you. For inspiration, check out the work of Maya Angelou, a poet, author, activist, and educator. Her poem "Phenomenal Woman," about loving your female form, can be found in her poetry collection of the same name.

TRUE STORY: Two Girls POISONED by Media Overload and LIVE to Tell About It!

Monique and Ines, both 14, are sitting at a crowded restaurant drinking sodas after dinner and talking nonstop about everything from the gangs in their neighborhood to their excitement and fears about starting high school in the fall. The conversation turns to what sports they might try out for (soccer tops the list) and Monique's dream of studying in Paris one day.

After dessert, they whip out two popular teen magazines, and their mood quickly changes. Monique and Ines study the pictures of tall, super skinny, glamorous models and celebrities with perfect hair, polished makeup, and pricey designer clothes. Though both girls have strong Latina pride and confidence in who they are, they start to slouch in their chairs with each flip of a page.

"I need to go to the gym more," Monique says under her breath.

"Yeah," Ines says, "I ate too much."

"I'm getting fat."

"Me too."

In a matter of magazine-browsing moments, they've gone from thinking about their futures to being disgusted with themselves. Monique and Ines are part of an epidemic: girls suffering from toxic media overload. The good news is that media overload can be treated. Read on to find out how you can build up your immunity to media toxins and spread the respect cure to girls everywhere.

4

Your Media IQ

Everywhere you turn you see magazines, TV shows, music videos, movies, games, ads, and Web sites. Media is always around and nearly impossible to tune out. But are media messages giving girls—no doubt one of the most powerful viewing audiences on the planet—the respect they deserve? All too often the answer is: Not even close.

This is not to say that media is all bad. Some media serves to inform, giving you the news you need to make educated decisions and understand the world. Most media targeted at girls, however, aims to entertain through fantasies that are passed off as fact. (Like articles and advertisements suggesting that if you change your look you'll get noticed by that special someone, or if you lose weight you'll be happier.) Media and advertising executives hope you'll buy into the fantasies—literally. These execs want to make cold hard cash off your desires and insecurities by selling you products. Companies spend $13 billion a year on ads and commercials directed at teens like you and your friends.[1] Marketers buy ad space in magazines, on TV, or on billboards so they can try to sell you all the makeup, styling products, and clothes that will supposedly make you picture-perfect.

Girls aren't only being encouraged to shop for perfection—they're also paying a heavy price when bombarded with images that are designed to sell an ideal lifestyle. Can you really be perfect? Nobody can. Should your only goal in life be to snag a guy? No way. Your self-respect can be affected by the relentless media messages that are a part of every girl's world. Many girls admit, and studies confirm, that they're influenced by media showing body standards, gender roles, and romantic relationships. Media and advertisers don't affect *your* ideals alone, however. They also have an impact on the standards of your friends, family members, and all the other people around you.

> Advertisements and Barbie dolls pollute our minds into thinking that we all have to have big breasts, a small waist, and a skinny figure. So everywhere you look, girls are trying to be perfect. But it gets tiring, and you wind up always looking down on yourself.
> —Molly, 15

> We're constantly being told we're not good enough—from clothes, to relationships, to what we do on the weekends. The media shows us that we have to be this cool, ultimate girl.
> —Karinna, 16

You still have a right to be different from media images and to question what you see and hear. And so you've got a choice to make: Are you going to be swayed by media messages and take them to heart, or will you be aware of them and decide for yourself what role they'll have in your life? We hope you'll seek the truth and won't buy in to toxic fantasies. You have the power to filter out the messages that bring you down, while keeping your eyes open for media that boosts your self-respect.

Popular FICTION

Many girls say they know that media influences how they feel about themselves—they just don't know how to stop it. So, where do you begin? First, you have to know when you're being sold a lie. Television and movie producers, as well as magazine publishers, often try to sell advertisers' products by getting you to believe these five major myths:

Myth 1: "You Can Never Be Too Thin or Too Pretty"

Whether she's posing for a magazine or star-ring in a blockbuster movie, the model-thin, drop-dead-gorgeous babe is the girl we're all supposed to admire and want to be like. It's her destiny to get whatever she wants in life—a hot guy, an awesome social life, and tons of attention. All you have to do is copy her look, including her body shape, and you'll be on the A-list, too.

THE TRUTH: With models plastered everywhere, it's no wonder that feelings of insecurity creep in when your own brand of beauty doesn't fit those narrow prototypes. And whose does? Advertisers bank on girls' self-doubts, and it seems to be working: Teenage girls and young women spend $4 billion annually on cosmetics and fashion alone, writes Jean Kilbourne in her book *Deadly Persuasion: Why Women and Girls Must Fight the Addictive Power of Advertising*. Among girls ages 15–18 who said they've taken diet pills, 73 percent are also frequent readers of women's health and fitness magazines.[2] From cover to cover, tons of magazines (and other media) sell you the myth that you *have* to be a certain kind of skinny and pretty to be accepted. By the way, all those perfect models get plenty of professional help to look the way they do!

When you don't accept yourself the way you are, you're more likely to go on risky diets, bash yourself, put down other girls, or try to get attention in ways that are harmful. It's easy to forget how great it feels to be appreciated and acknowledged for your brains, creativity, and spirit—qualities that are so much more important than what you've got on the outside.

> I know in real life the actress or model probably has crooked teeth, red eyes, and a lot more fat than we'll ever see on the pages of a magazine, but I still feel the need to live up to that airbrushed perfection. And that makes me be hard on myself.
>
> —Ana, 17

Teen-Girl-Magazine Editors
TELL ALL!

Top editors from two of the world's biggest teen magazines have one thing to tell you about the media: You're not supposed to believe everything you read or see. These women know the magazine world inside and out, and they decided to share top secrets so girls can blow the lid off the myths once and for all.

Q. Why do girls in the magazines always look perfect?

A. The dirty secret about magazines is that we're making a fantasy image. Also, the faces, arms, and legs look so silky smooth and flawless in magazine photos because the models/celebs have professional makeup artists, and then get totally made over with airbrushing and other nifty fixes in a photo-editing computer program. Plus, lighting experts come in and make sure the shot is perfect to make them look extra good. You can turn a gorilla into a Hollywood starlet with enough photo editing! Girls should see magazines as a way to get ideas, and view the photos for inspiration (not imitate them).

Q. Clothes fit just right on models and celebs, and their hair is flawless. What's their secret?

A. Well, for photos and movie shoots, clothes often are pinned up or taped in the back and on the sides. Either you can't see these temporary alterations, or they get removed during the editing process. Many of the little how-to articles for hairstyles aren't really that practical either. All of the featured models have professional hairstylists do their hair just for the shoot. And celebs get the same treatment for photo shoots at their houses, where they are supposedly "keeping it real" and just hanging out. So, when you compare yourself to these pictures, remember that from their heads to their toes these women and girls get "made up," literally.

Q. What kinds of stories or ads do you think can eat away at a girl's self-respect?

A. It's true that teen magazines will have cover lines like, "How to Tell If Your Best Friend Is Anorexic," or "Has Extreme Dieting Hit Your Crowd?" These stories can actually be thinly veiled "how-to" pieces about how to diet. Even though they *seem* to be about a danger that's out there, in a way these articles can make eating disorders seem cool, trendy, or like an effective way to lose weight. As a society, we've become more diverse but our ideal of beauty has actually become narrower—and skinnier.

Still, it's not fair to think that magazines are all to blame for the objectification of young girls—just watch TV. Some magazines, like the ones we work for now, try to strike a balance between journalistic stories and fantasy, don't allow advertisements for diet pills or breast enlargements, and look for models who aren't too skinny (if a model is too skinny, we'll turn her away at the casting call).

Q. Why don't magazines feature real girls on their covers?

A. Readers say, "I want to see a real girl on the cover." But it also seems like it's a part of human nature to want to see beautiful things—and beauty is what does sell off the racks. Plus, more and more celebrities are put on covers because their publicists make deals with magazines. Actresses are usually on a cover around the same time that one of their movies is coming out, or because their publicity team is trying to make them an "it girl."

Q. Why do a lot of girls want to be models?

A. Girls may want to be models just because they're skinny and get to wear nice clothes. The fact is that many models don't make a lot of money, finish high school, or go to college. It's not as glamorous as it seems. The career length of the average model is, like, three years.

Q. In this media-crazed world, how can girls keep building respect for themselves?

A. The coolest girls we meet have outside interests. They watch old movies, make their own clothes, and listen to alternative music—they respect themselves as individuals and aren't being part of the herd. They're not worried about what other people think. You have to be smart enough to know when a group is good for you or not. Choose who you hang out with wisely and learn to do stuff on your own. Girls are smart enough to know a bad situation from a good one. Self-respect is about not being afraid to say what matters to you and what you want. Practice saying no. It's like the reverse of the Nike ad: "Just *Don't* Do It."

reTroSPECT:
MerCHaNTS OF "COOL"

Cool doesn't just happen. It's often calculated and created by corporate marketing campaigns (advertising and promotion). For example, despite heavy criticism, some tobacco and alcohol companies still target teens with messages about how to be "cool"—implying that teens should consume their products long before they're old enough to actually buy them.

Case in point: Alcohol companies reportedly spent more than $590 million on national magazine ads in 2001 and 2002, and most of the ads were geared toward teen girls.[3] Why would these companies target you with ads when it's illegal for you to consume alcohol, and when drinking is known to increase the risks of driving-accident deaths, sexual behavior, and suicide attempts? The answer: money. And many companies don't only want a slice of your allowance *today*. They want to "brand" you now, when you're young, so you'll prefer their products when you're older. It's what they call brand loyalty, and they want yours as soon as you can read an ad or watch one on TV.

Myth 2: "You *Must* Be Popular"

With a hip makeover, a movie's intelligent outcast can be transformed overnight into a popular girl who quickly becomes part of the crew that rules the school. To be cookie-cutter popular, all you need to do is get the right look, compete with other girls for status, or be loved (or feared) by everyone.

THE TRUTH: Most girls don't look like, act like, or have the lifestyles of popular girls in media or on so-called "reality TV." Yet, many girls want to fit in based on what they see, and advertisers and product-makers know this. They'll pay big bucks for ads in magazines, TV commercials that play during your favorite shows, and product placements in teen movies. (When you see an actress carting around a mega-expensive handbag on the screen and you can clearly read the label, that could be a product placement.) Companies even hire teens as consultants to *start* trends by having them use their products or wear their brands.

Advertisers *want you* to want to fit in at any cost. Girls are sent a message that having the "right stuff"—clothes, makeup, gadgets, accessories, or even an extravagant sweet 16 party—will put you at the top of the popularity list. So, while you're being entertained or informed by magazines and movies, you're also being slyly manipulated to go and buy a bunch of loot. And look at what's being sold to make you seem cool: often, it's revealing clothing, alcohol, and cigarettes. And what's being pitched to make you look rich? Brands so pricey that the cost of a shirt could suck up a year's allowance.

We all know girls who are popular among their friends and totally themselves, but whose assets aren't counted in dollars. Their secret? Self-respect. Trying to buy your way to popularity won't raise your level of respect. If you strive for the media definition of popularity, then you'll probably have to go against your gut, your boundaries, and who you really are. Wouldn't you rather gain friends and admirers based on the *real* you?

Myth 3: "You Need to Find Mr. Right"

From movies to books to magazines, the story is the same from the time a girl heads off to kindergarten: Get a guy or else forget about happily ever after. Love is only love if you're swept off your feet by Prince Charming, lavished with gifts and compliments, or caught up in some major dramas, like breaking up and making up all the time.

SISTERHOOD

Today's media seems fixated on storylines about "mean girls." By promoting images of popular girls as snotty hotties who get treated like goddesses, the media spreads the myth that popular equals *mean*. But this isn't true. There are plenty of well-liked girls who aren't rude to other girls. True popularity—a.k.a. having lots of meaningful friendships—comes from being supportive of other girls, not competing with them.

THE TRUTH: There's absolutely nothing wrong with wanting to fall in love. But books and magazines often spread the message that you've got to be a part of a couple to be happy. Teen magazine articles reinforce the importance of getting a guy by focusing much more on dating (35 percent of their articles) than on subjects like school or careers (12 percent).[4] And across a range of media, females are portrayed as intent on finding Mr. Right. (Forget about girls who love girls— 99 percent of all primetime characters are heterosexual, after all.)[5] On TV and in movies, women are represented as wanting to have a romantic relationship more often than men are.[6]

There is so much more to a girl's life than finding a guy. And how are you sup- posed to feel about this "boy-plus-girl-equals-happiness" message if you don't even like guys, are bisexual, or are questioning your sexual identity? True, many teen girls *are* looking for love, thanks to surging hormones and a budding interest in re- lationships. But at a time in your life when you're still figuring out who *you* are and what you want, your attention is often redirected to how you can get the attention of the opposite sex. If you're led to believe that love is a perfect fairytale that goes off without a hitch, you can quickly become dissatisfied when this dream doesn't come true or doesn't play out the way it does on the big screen.

Believe it or not, your personal passions can be more satisfying than romantic attention. When you're a self-respecting girl, you're more attractive, interesting, mature, and relationship-ready anyway. And that feels better than spending time feeling awful when a crush hasn't noticed you or made all your dreams come true. You've got the power to make your own dreams come true!

Big Sis Wisdom:
The Truth About
"Happily Ever After"

Rachel Safier remembers the first romantic movie she ever saw as a young girl. She was mesmerized when a happy couple walked off into the clouds (which seemed even more romantic than walking off into the sunset). From that point on, Rachel, like a lot of girls, got many more doses of fairytale romance.

Fast forward to just before Rachel's real-life wedding. Everything seemed perfect: the proposal, the dress, and the guy. Two weeks before Rachel was going to say "I do," however, she called off the wedding when her fiancé pressed her about her doubts. Getting married just wasn't right for her at that time, and she knew it.

Rachel has since interviewed hundreds of other runaway brides, and she tells their stories in her book, *There Goes the Bride: Making Up Your Mind, Calling It Off, and Moving On*. What did the "almost brides" all have in common? Deep down they believed what they'd learned from media: that "The One" was out there, and a girl could only be happy when she found him.

Today, Rachel says that she didn't listen to her gut when it was telling her she wasn't ready for marriage. She ignored the migraines and stomachaches that started right after accepting the proposal. Why did she ignore those signals? She says it was the influence of all those Cinderella stories she'd heard and seen over the years. Although she wanted to believe in her own fairytale, her gut was telling her a different story.

"Women often have an idea from childhood and teenage-hood that a guy—Prince Charming or Mr. Right—will save them and take care of them, and that the marriage proposal has to be the most romantic and happiest time of their life," Rachel says. "There is this pounding voice in your head saying that if you don't want to get married in a really romantic way, something is wrong with you—and that idea is promoted by movies, magazines, and commercials. Even if you think you know better, this happily-ever-after programming is planted deep inside your brain."

Myth 4: "Life Is Super Sexy"

Everywhere you look on TV and in movies, things are getting hot and heavy. Teens tear each other's clothes off to hook up, and make-out sessions are just part of the scenery. Sex hardly ever involves a conversation, before or after. And when people aren't doing it, they're alluding to it in really clever ways.

THE TRUTH: The media routinely shows hookups that are nothing but fantasy, and sometimes it can be difficult to distinguish life on the screen from the real thing. Researchers have found that the majority of TV movies, sitcoms, and soaps have sexual content.[7] Teens who watch television shows that portray sexual situations are twice as likely to have sex as teens who don't watch those programs.[8] What's the underlying message of many TV shows and movies? That sex is a risk-free rite of passage during the teen years, and that you have to do it to prove you're mature and sexy. *So* not true.

Watching fictitious sex can't prepare you for the real thing. That's because love scenes on TV or in movies are choreographed and stylized, making them seem perfect. These fantasies can set you up for false expectations. If a romantic encounter doesn't go the way you've seen it on the screen (and it rarely does), then you might freeze up and not speak up when you're in an actual situation. And you may be less likely to check your gut or tell the other person your boundaries.

Myth 5: "Females Are Eye Candy or Victims"

Young women enjoy wearing next to nothing (and have nothing better to do than grind up against some guy in a music video). Women can only report the news when they're all glammed up. And females are always the star victims of the latest slasher flick.

THE TRUTH: In the entertainment world, women and teen girls have always played the roles of pretty props or damsels in distress. And have you noticed the sheer number of smart, talented female celebrities who *still* package themselves as sex objects to get noticed? A lot of girls look up to media idols and mimic their behavior, without making the connection that the vixen routine is a ticket-selling act for that celeb.

On a magazine cover, the first thing you see is an unrealistically beautiful girl. The second thing is "How to get that guy." And the next thing is "How to look good." Every human craves acceptance. If you see these images all the time, you start to believe that's the only way to be accepted, which is a lie.—Malika, 16

When girls and women are portrayed as sex objects or victims, it can make them seem like they're less human—and that fuels real-life disrespect. The bottom line is that most media and entertainment companies still promote the idea that violence against females sells, and that sex sells even better. But when girls and women are portrayed as victims, it's especially dangerous: More than 3,500 studies have looked at how media violence is connected to violent behavior in the real world, and all except 18 of the reports showed a link between what people see and how they act it out in real life.[9]

Media images have some effect on you, no matter how sharp you are. This doesn't mean you're powerless, though. You definitely don't have to buy into the hype. Ultimately, *you* get to decide where your money goes. You can support media that shows strong, smart, and powerful women.

TAKE BACK the Media

There's no question that girls are intelligent. And most of us know that too many fake images and storylines—like too much candy or sun—can be bad for your system. So, how can you start to filter your media intake so you can still be entertained but not get caught up in the myths? By flexing your economic and intellectual power. Try the following activities to raise your media IQ and your self-respect.

Question What You See

Media and entertainment company executives would shake in their boots if girls like you started picking apart their content and calling their bluff. Take a fresh look at your favorite shows, magazines, and ads to discover the myths they want you to fall for. Decide to make savvier media choices instead.

Look for stereotypes and myths. Spend a day or two looking for stereotypes of females in movies, on TV, in videos, and in other media. For example, keep an eye out for programs or content that includes women and girls who are dressed sexy *all* the time, girls fighting with other girls over guys, and girls who act clueless or helpless. When you've had your fill, think about what bothered you. What did the images tell you about respect?

They have so much beauty crap in magazines. I don't like it because I don't wear makeup. It's propaganda. I'd rather read the letters and true stories.
—Ally, 15

Although these images can affect how the world views girls (and their capabilities), you still have the power to tune them out. You can always make the choice to question what you see, and when you do, you'll feel more empowered. Remind yourself on a daily basis that stereotypes don't reflect what's going on in the real world.

Look for real females. While you're noticing stereotypes or myths, also watch for *real* role models on TV or in movies, such as women and girls who break the mold because they are:

- not wearing makeup or designer clothes

- not only interested in romance

- from diverse racial backgrounds

- single *and* happy

- smart, independent, and strong

- confident in business or school settings, without downplaying their talents

- proud of their unique style or womanly body

- going for goals that aren't stereotypically female

- serious, without being apologetic

When you see self-respecting female characters or entertainers in action, stop and take notice. Think about what they represent and how they can be role models for you and other girls.

Look for motives. Dig a little deeper by asking yourself these questions:

- Who created the show, ad, or publication? Is a brand name or company being promoted or listed anywhere? Or is a political or religious group behind it?

- Why was the media created? To sell something, like a product? To educate you about a problem or political issue? To convince you of a point of view?

✤ What do the media creators want? Do they want you to just "buy" the media (like a ticket to a movie) to make money off the sale? Are you being persuaded to purchase a product or give a donation? Or being counted for ratings, which in turn helps TV shows get more money out of advertisers?

Once you've questioned what you see for a day or two, you'll learn a lot about what you're consuming. But the ultimate goal is to question the media you see and hear *every* day. Your mind and body are yours to protect and take care of—don't let anything in without thinking twice about what you're learning, absorbing, and being led to believe.

Make Over Your Media

After you've taken a closer look at your favorite media to find stereotypes, go on a media "fast" to see if you can feel the difference. A fast lets you detox from disrespectful media, while helping you learn how these messages make you feel inside. Here's how to do it:

1. Take inventory. List all the media you absorb each week, including TV, movies, books, magazines, music videos, and Web sites, as well as ads at bus stops, on billboards, or at mall kiosks.

2. Journal. Before your fast, answer the following questions in your journal:

✤ What do you like about your body and mind?

✤ What's on your shopping wish list?

✤ What would make you most happy right now?

✤ What do you worry about?

3. Fast. Start your media fast. For a week or two, cut out the media that you consume the most—like TV or magazines.

4. Check in. At the end of your media fast, pull out your journal and answer the above list of questions again. Then answer these questions:

✤ Do you notice any difference between how you felt about yourself before the fast and how you feel now?

✤ Do you see any changes in your body image, worries, and desires?

If you're tuned in to how certain media myths and messages affect your self-respect, you can start to filter these toxins so they no longer influence you as much. To put your media IQ to work:

Make a ditch list. What media do you want to ditch entirely? Is there a magazine or program that's particularly offensive, now that you've taken a closer look at its messages? You can stop buying it and start finding media that helps you feel good.

Set your filters. Maybe you have a favorite show or movie that has an offensive character or myth in it, but you don't want to stop watching it altogether. That's where a filter comes in handy. Identify the myth or stereotype that bothers you—say it out loud while you're watching or write about it in your journal. What's harmful about the message? Think about how you'd change the script or media message to make it more respectful.

Take it further. You can make your filters even stronger by cutting offensive ads out of magazines, stepping out of the room during commercials, or recording TV shows and fast-forwarding through the ads.

Go to the Source

If you want to see more respectful images of young women, then take your case to the source. You can start a letter-writing or email campaign to pressure the makers of a certain show, product, or magazine to portray girls in a more respectful light.

In your letter or email, make a point of giving specific examples of how the material is disrespectful to its core audience (you!). Then offer examples of what you'd like to see instead. To find the address of a magazine, look in the opening pages where the masthead—the list of editors and staff—is located. You can find the address of a company or manufacturer on the product label itself or by doing an Internet search.

You could also send letters and emails showing your support. For example, if you find movies and TV shows with female characters you admire, you might applaud the studios (and actresses) with some fan mail and tell them what they're doing right. To find a studio address or a celebrity's contact information, use the Internet or do some research at the library.

Let Your Wallet Do the Talking

Media and entertainment companies won't keep creating content that no one wants to see—there's no money in that. If you're tired of disrespectful messages from certain performers and companies, then you can refuse to shell out your cash to support them.

To send a louder message, gather your friends and other girls, and stage a full-scale boycott (meaning you refuse to buy the products or messages anymore). Make sure to let your targets know that you're rejecting their products or programming until they make some changes. And call a few local news stations or reporters to cover your boycott. You can find news producers' or reporters' numbers in the phone book or on their corporate Web site. Fax them a press release that states the details (who, what, where, when, and why) of your boycott. For more activism ideas, including other ways to make your voice heard, check out Chapter 12.

Throw a Media Critic Party

You and your friends are the best critics you know, right? So, during your next get-together or sleepover, play this game to take a fresh look at your favorite media—and discover the fiction being passed off as fact. Choose your favorite magazine, TV show, or movie and designate someone to make a note of every time you see a girl or woman who represents a myth or stereotype. Afterward, look at the list. What did you see that bugged you? What made you feel angry or insecure? What images and ideas were respectful to girls and women (if any)? If you're feeling fired up, consider writing a letter to the producer of the show or movie, or to the magazine editors.

Do It Yourself

Have you ever thought about creating your own media as an alternative to what's out there? Imagine what you'd like to read, view, and listen to that's more respectful of girls—then venture into do-it-yourself media by getting your voice and POV into the mix:

Contribute stories. Find magazines that represent real girls and pitch them an article. For example, *Teen Voices* (see page 214) is produced by girls who write savvy articles about their world. To try to get published in a magazine, write a quick summary of your proposed article, making sure to start your pitch (or query letter) with a catchy paragraph that identifies a problem or your take on a news trend. Then send it to the magazine's main editor and see what happens.

Get creative. More and more young women are becoming film directors, music producers, and record-label owners. You can record your own songs or edit digital film on most computers these days. You can even start your own talk show on public access cable. And you don't need tons of cash to start your own Web site, blog, or zine that talks about your life and the issues that you and your friends deal with, along with girls' success stories. Send the link to friends and try to get the traditional media to write about your indie project for publicity and to drive people to your site.

Check it out. The Center for Media Literacy (www.medialit.org) has tons of how-tos on creating your own media, from magazines to documentaries and news programs. For DIY tips, see the Media section of "More Info" on pages 213–214.

Girl Media Mavericks

These girls took the DIY approach (and you've gotta respect them for that!).

Real-world comics:

When Ariel Schrag started high school, she wanted to document what was really going on, while expressing her passion for comic artistry. Her idea? Become a publisher. Ariel began chronicling her life at Berkeley High School in California. In a series of comic books, Ariel depicted her firsthand experiences with friends, sexual identity, school, and experimentation. At 15, Ariel self-published her first comic book, *Awkward,* and then got a publishing contract for her follow-ups, *Definition* and *Potential.* Ariel's work tells the unedited truth about her life in high school, and the ups and downs of growing up. When she gained national media attention, girls everywhere heard about her work.

All-girl radio:

When a group of girls from Boston got tired of hearing songs about women as sex objects or victims, they decided to take action. They came up with the idea of creating a radio station by and for girls. With some help from a youth media organization, they took their case all the way to the city mayor. The mayor was impressed, and the girls were given the green light to set up their radio station, R-LOG (540 AM), which they operate from their school. For three hours each day, R-LOG spins records that don't slam women, and conducts interviews and phone-ins about issues girls care about. The station's motto says it all:

"Where the voices of young women are heard and respected."

Part Two:

Getting
and Giving
Respect

Making Respect a Family Affair

Ever wonder what makes a relationship between a teen girl and her parent respectful? Andrea Frank Henkart and her teen daughter, Journey, know: They're the coauthors of *Cool Communication,* a book about how teens and parents can improve how they relate to each other.

Q. What's the first step in having a trusting relationship with your parents?

Andrea: You've got to understand your differences. As parents, we have spent many years taking care of our children, and we get upset sometimes because we're afraid of what will happen if we give up control. But most of the time, parents are coming from a place of profound love.

Journey: When kids feel controlled, sometimes they rebel or don't communicate because they don't feel trusted.

Q. What's the best way for girls to bring up their feelings?

Journey: Find the right time to talk. If you're in public or in the middle of an argument, wait and make an "appointment" to talk later. When you do talk, get your message across by owning your feelings and being aware of your body language. Have conversations where you don't yell—you listen and you compromise.

Q. How can girls keep the respect going in their families?

Andrea: When you're talking with your parents, just remember that their concerns as a mom or dad are going to be different from your concerns right now.

Journey: Sometimes, we use our power to make our parents angry. Use your power for something more positive: to communicate. Your parents will have more confidence in you, and you'll get more freedom and respect.

5

Family

Here's something that's true for most girls: You want to feel loved and accepted by your family. No matter what your home life is like, chances are your heart is connected to your family (or wants to be) because your family is a part of you. How your family interacts can set you up for a life filled with respect—or time spent dealing with old hurts and a list of unhealthy habits to break. And this is why striving for respect between you and your family is so necessary, right now and always.

Families come in all shapes and sizes. You might have a bunch of siblings or none. You might live with a mother and father, a parent and stepparent, one parent, or a legal guardian like a grandparent, an aunt, an older sibling, or a foster parent. Your parents might be the same sex, or you might live with a group of adults—some related and others not—who are committed to raising you. For the sake of simplicity, we mainly use the terms "parent" and "parents" to describe who's responsible for caring for you. If that terminology doesn't apply to you, you have the smarts to fill in what does and to figure out how the family situations we describe apply to your life.

In an ideal world, you'd live with family members who have healthy relationships and who love you unconditionally. They'd trust you, support you in all your interests, listen to you, encourage you to be independent, and lend a shoulder to cry on when you're down. You, in return, would be respectful of their needs, open and honest, always grateful for what they've given you, and understanding of what they have to say. But the world isn't this simple for every girl and parent. Families are complicated. And so is your quest for independence and trust while you're growing up.

> My mother, her partner, and my father all respect me as a person who deserves to be heard. My mother talks to me like I'm an equal, and her partner tells me stories of her homeland and listens to my opinion on the problems happening there. My father takes me seriously and respects what I have to say, even if we disagree.
> —Adelina, 15

I think it's hard for parents to respect their kids when they start to grow up because they had a certain vision of how their child would turn out, and it's hard to see that vision not being fulfilled. There's probably no parent in the history of forever that ever saw their daughter grow up just the way they envisioned she would!

—Ani, 17

No matter how old you are, you're becoming more independent every day. You might be deciding what you want and how to get it for the first time in your life. Or figuring out how you want to be different from your parents and recognizing that you don't agree with all of their views and values. You're also learning about your power: how you can influence others, express anger or rebel, and meet many of your own needs. These are all big changes for you and your parents. As you assert your independence, your parents will probably struggle with how much to protect you, trust you, and let you go.

Even without these struggles, respect is on the line in any family. You might be too busy to show each other basic consideration (like saying "please" and "thank you"). Sometimes, the family leaders—a.k.a. parents—haven't learned that respect is a family value, and they set poor examples (such as name-calling or arguing all the time). If it seems like your home got skipped when the universe was handing out respect, it doesn't have to be this way forever. You can help your family learn to be more respectful. You can lead by example by treating others well. And you can keep caring for yourself at times when you don't get the respect you deserve.

Communication 101

At this time in your life, communication problems may surface like never before. That's because as you start to gain more independence, you and your parents won't always see eye to eye about how you're growing up. Even if you're mature and you've proven that you're responsible, your mom or dad still might set limits that you think are unfair. Or you might make a mistake (or cross a line) that spurs your parents to tighten the reins and pull back their trust.

And speaking of trust, sometimes it may seem like your parents call all the shots and you have no say in what you do or where you go—and maybe this is actually

My family shows respect in the way we talk to each other and by respecting each other's privacy. If my parents didn't love each other as much as they do and show us that family comes first, we wouldn't be who we are. Their honesty and support keeps us strong.—Winter, 16

the case. You and your parents may have major conflicts over issues like dating, grades, chores, and your future. These power struggles can lead to frustration or arguments. At times, it may seem like your family goes from talking, to debating, to fighting in a minute flat. When you stop listening and start yelling, disrespect can take over your home.

Believe it or not, your dad or mom might be going through some of the same emotional ups and downs you are. You're becoming even more of an individual, and your parents might feel like you don't need them as much. In their eyes, only yesterday you were playing in puddles and now maybe you want to play in a band or go on the road with one. Your parents will probably set more boundaries to protect you. This can put a strain on your relationship (not to mention on the rest of the family, if the sparks are flying all the time).

So, how can you keep the respect going *and* become more independent? For starters, remember that when it comes to respect you get what you give. Even though your parents are in charge (hey, it's their legal obligation), you can take the lead on the respect front in terms of your behavior and choices.

Tip: Set an Example

Having respectful relationships with your family doesn't mean you all act like best friends. Respect is shown in how you communicate and care for one another. Like when your parents or siblings listen to your opinions, even if they disagree. When they support your rights. And when they treat you like the mature person you're becoming.

In return, you can listen to your parents' or siblings' views and acknowledge their right to have different opinions. If they tell you that something you've done has hurt them, you can listen and apologize. If family members mention something they'd like you to work on, you can hear them out. You can also show basic consideration by not treating your home like a hotel with maid service or expecting your parents to drop everything the moment you need a ride. This will help make your transition to adulthood a lot smoother!

If it's independence you're after, your days of getting things handed to you or done for you are numbered. For some girls, this has never been an issue—you may have been doing your own laundry since you were old enough to pick up

Even when I have problems that make my mom upset, she still talks to me like a friend. She always has time for me, even if she's tired or it's a really small problem. That makes me feel like she really cares about me.—Jen, 13

a bottle of detergent. But for others, it may be the norm to rely on the adults in the family to do most of the cleaning and other tasks. The best way to prove you can handle your independence is by taking your family and household responsibilities to heart. You might do more chores or get an after-school job to help pay for some of your expenses—food and toiletry costs add up. Even if you don't volunteer to do more, you can show maturity by keeping the agreements you've already made with your family. Honoring your agreements shows respect.

Draft Respectful Family Rules

If you want to be a respect leader at home, think of your family as members of the United Nations and call a meeting to address any issues. You may all represent different interests and want different things, but you also share a household and responsibilities. So, doesn't it make sense for all of you to work together on drafting some respect rules for everyone to follow? Start by answering these questions:

1. What is our definition of respect?

2. How will we show respect to one another?

3. What disrespectful behaviors are considered unacceptable in our home?

4. How will we respond to them?

When your family writes the final list of rules, everyone can sign it and promise to uphold respect.

Tip: Talk the Talk

How you and your family members speak to each other is where respect can begin—and end. Let's face it, though: Talking about certain issues with a parent can be downright difficult. You're still living by adult rules at a time when you're becoming a young woman who has her own point of view (POV). If your parents already listen to you—or at least seem willing to try—then open up. Talking will get you so much further than silence will.

Start a dialogue. When you want to ask for something, the goal is to have a calm two-way conversation so everyone has a say. Here's how:

1. Think about what you want and why. More space for alone time? A later curfew? Say it in your mind first so the words come out the way you want them to.

2. Choose your **tone of voice** and **body language** carefully. If your hands are on your hips and you sigh, roll your eyes, or stomp around, the conversation may quickly turn into an argument.

3. When a parent is talking, **listen.** Try not to think only about your next comeback or interrupt with your POV.

4. Let people know you've heard their message. Try, "I see what you're saying," or "You've got a good point."

5. Compromise, if necessary. Give in a little to get some of what you want.

Start fresh. If you've let family members down or you've been in major conflicts, it will take time to build trust. To smooth the way, you might try, "A lot has happened, and you've lost some trust in me. I want to start over and work stuff out. Can we talk about it?" You also need to *show* that you can be trusted. So follow the rules and prove that you take your role in the family seriously. You know the saying: Actions speak louder than words.

My parents let me do stuff for myself. They let me learn from my own experiences, so I can build my own opinions on who I am and how I want people to treat me.
—Rosalie, 15

Tell it like it is. Do your parents know what you need? We're not talking about your birthday wish list, but what you *really* need on your way to independence. More responsibility? Fewer limitations? Take some time to lay everything out on the table. Be specific so they know what privileges you want and are willing to earn.

My family members listen to my opinions and ideas. They don't tell me that my feelings are stupid, and they don't underestimate me because of my gender. They are proud of me and they support me, and this shows that they have respect for me.—Steph, 14

Tell the truth. If there's one surefire way to lose a parent's trust, it's by lying. You might feel like you need to lie to keep the peace, keep your sanity, or get your way, but lying only creates more problems. Your family members could lose their faith in you, and you could lose your privileges. And that will put a bigger clamp on your independence.

Tip: Try to Understand

Here's some advice that will never fail in life: Know who you're talking to. To have a stronger relationship with your family members, especially the adults, it helps to try to understand where they're coming from. Parents realize that they grew up in a different time than you, but it wasn't in the age of the dinosaurs. There's some common ground between you, and they probably remember the days when it seemed like *their* parents were from a different century. Here's what you can do:

Bridge the gap. When there's a generation gap, it can seem like it's impossible to relate to each other (it's not!). To help close the gap, let your parents know about the pressures you're under and what's really going on in your world. If you paint a clear picture, they'll probably be able to relate.

Get the scoop. Have you ever *asked* the adults in your family what life was like for them when they were your age? They might come clean about some stuff that will make them seem more human or (gasp!) even cool. Without realizing it, many adults repeat the parenting they experienced as children—the good, the so-so, and the unhealthy. By learning more about how your parents were raised, you can start to build a better relationship with them.

What Was It Like Back Then?

Want to dig up some juicy details about the adults in your family? Now's your chance. Interview them about their teen years. When they talk about themselves and the feelings they had at your age, they'll probably see more clearly why you act a certain way (as well as why *they* do). Ask questions like:

- What was going on in the world when you were my age?

- Did you feel pressure to do certain things or be a certain kind of person—like what?

- What kinds of mistakes did you make? What did you learn?

- What was your relationship like with your parents?

- What kinds of rules and privileges did you have?

- How did your family deal with conflicts? Do you think that worked well?

- How has the way you were raised influenced how you're raising me?

Get their POV. If you want your parents to consider your thoughts and needs, you have to do the same for them. Try a little understanding by saying, "Yeah, I think I see what you mean," or "I can see how you would feel that way." Being able to get a parent's POV—even when you don't agree with it—shows maturity.

Get to their fears. Some parents are really protective, which can create major growing pains as you try to become more independent. One way to ease the pain is to understand *why* they're so protective. Adults invest a lot in their parenting—hey, raising kids is hard work! Try saying, "I understand that you want to protect me, but I'm not totally clear on what you think might happen. Can you tell me?" Listen closely. Their fears are clues to how you can negotiate what you want. If they're worried you'll get physically hurt, how can you assure them that you'll be safe? Gently let them know that, while you understand, they're going to have to ease up eventually. You might say, "I'm getting older, and I need some more space. Can you let me try _____, and we can see how it goes?"

Say thanks. Just like you, your parents (and siblings) need to hear when you think they've done well. Let them know when they're doing a great job by complimenting their parenting, their skills, or the choices they're making in life. When they do something you appreciate, tell them so. It can go a long way to say, "Dad, I really like it when you listen to me—thanks!"

Tip: Keep Your Cool

Many girls say that strong emotions bubble up every day, making them want to scream at the first family member in sight. Other girls bury their feelings deep inside. No matter how you've handled anger, frustration, or disappointment in the past, it has probably come out in some way on the home front because family members are easy targets when those bottled-up feelings erupt.

When you feel a conflict brewing, you don't have to turn the other cheek—but you can turn up the respect. That's not always easy to do when disagreements get heated. Even though you can't always control how family members treat you, you can control your reactions by trying these ideas:

Breathe through it. During conflicts, most people start showing signs of stress (sweating, a pounding heart). This may sound *too* easy, but right when you feel yourself getting upset, focus on your breathing. Take a few deep breaths to stay cool—the extra oxygen can help your body calm down.

Feel it. Just because you're trying to stay calm doesn't mean you have to hold in your feelings or push them away. Recognize your feelings in your own mind.

Hear it. During a conflict, it sometimes helps to listen more than you talk. What is the other person really feeling? How do you wish things would turn out? What do you both want? Is there a way to compromise?

Hold it. Sometimes, it's hard to resist the impulse to push a family member's buttons. But pushing buttons is a power play to get a reaction. The conflict intensifies, making it more difficult to resolve. So, even when you know just which buttons to push, tell yourself that you can find a better way to communicate your needs.

Say it. At times when you disagree, be sure to minimize the eye rolling or door slamming. Instead, ask if you can talk about what's bothering you. Start by sharing how you feel, what you'd like to have happen, and why. Be aware of when you might

need to excuse yourself from the discussion. If you're too upset and you're starting to yell, ask to take a break and pick up where you left off later (try some deep breathing in the meantime).

Admit it. During a conflict, you might need to admit when you've done something hurtful, which can be difficult for anyone. Don't just give a brief, under-the-breath "Sorry" and leave it at that. Instead, be more sincere and say something like, "I feel so bad about when I yelled at you, and I regret it because I know I hurt your feelings. I'm really sorry." Apologizing in a heartfelt way shows you care. Forgive yourself, too, and make it your goal to avoid the same behavior next time.

Think on it. Even if a conflict was resolved peacefully, take some time to think about what went down. Is anything still bugging you? What do you wish you'd have done differently? Is there something you need to discuss with the family member in question, like how you were treated or how you'd like the person to communicate with you in the future? Break out your journal and write down your thoughts.

Bound-a-ries, Please

Many families don't hold back—they just let their words fly, especially when it comes to criticism. When people who are supposed to love you are harsh, their words tend to hurt (and stick). The same goes for you if you're dishing out criticism to a parent or sibling. If one of your family members harshly criticizes you, filter it. Here's how:

❧ First, try not to take immediate offense. Stop and ask yourself, "Is there some truth to that?" Feedback from other people helps you grow. So, in your mind, take the good ("Do I need to work on _____?") but leave the bad ("The way she said that was rude. She didn't need to say _____").

❧ Next, tell the person how you feel. Try, "I appreciate your concern, but the way you said it hurt my feelings. Next time, could you try to tell me what I need to work on without saying _____?"

Tip: Don't Demand, Do Negotiate

In any conversation or conflict, negotiation can come in handy. When you negotiate, you work to keep the scale balanced and to compromise. Learning to negotiate is one of the keys to earning the trust and independence you want. Here are a few do's and don'ts to remember:

❧ **Do pick your battles (wisely).** One of the biggest complaints parents have about their teen daughters is that everything is an argument. If that's the case in your family, take a closer look at what your arguments are about. Do you complain about nitpicky stuff (like your dad always listens to *his* radio station in the car)? Sometimes, you'll have to let things go or agree to disagree. If you focus on the bigger issues, like new freedoms you want, the adults in your family will have more energy to negotiate about what really matters.

❧ **Do choose a good time.** You don't want to talk about a touchy subject with your mom when she just got home from a tough day at work, was stuck in traffic, and now has to pay the bills. And you especially don't want to start in when you *just* got busted for something or didn't fulfill an obligation. Wait until everyone is calm and in a good mood.

❧ **Don't jump to conclusions.** If you assume you know exactly how a parent or sibling will react to what you're saying, you're not being open to new possibilities or to compromise. Enter every negotiation with an open heart and mind. Don't expect to get *everything* you want right away. Be willing to listen and to find a middle ground.

❧ **Do watch your body language.** To show respect, make eye contact with the person you're talking to. Nod your head, maybe say "Uh-huh" every once in a while to show you're listening, and never have your arms crossed (because you'll look defensive or bored). If a family member isn't listening to you or seems uncomfortable, ask a question to loosen things up. Try, "Do you know what I mean?"

❧ **Do start with how you feel.** When you're negotiating, it helps to start your conversations with how you feel instead of what you want. ("I feel _____ when you _____.") Then say how you'd like things to change or what you need—that's when the real negotiating begins.

❧ **Don't refuse to take no for an answer.** The truth about negotiating is that you can't always get what you want—both sides need to give a little. Hearing

"No" or "Not now" can be a downer, but it's the perfect time *not* to blow up. If you can handle setbacks maturely, your parents will notice. And if you respect their limits, your parents will be more likely to negotiate with you again.

Creating a respectful relationship with your family will take time and effort. Most likely, you'll have to work on it for the rest of your lives. Be patient and keep at it, and you'll make progress one step (or calm conversation) at a time. If the adults in your family refuse to give communication and negotiation a try, remember that you won't be under their roof *forever*—there is light at the end of the tunnel!

BARELY Relating

Your parents' needs probably aren't that different from your own: You want to be heard, appreciated, understood, listened to, and loved for who you are. What sets you and your parents apart is that they're adults, and they need to be a positive example to help you become a strong and healthy young woman. How they treat you while you're growing up shapes how you see the world, think, and behave.

To raise the respect level in your family, think about your rights. Are they being overlooked or ignored? Are you getting what you need? You have to acknowledge when your family doesn't show you respect, or it can be tough for you to respect yourself or get it from others.

Your right: To be different from your family.

Your right disrespected: When your parents want to mold you into mini versions of themselves. When you're not allowed to have ideas that differ from your family's beliefs about religion, politics, or rules. When you're criticized for looking or acting different from the rest of your family. When family members tell you not to embarrass them, or they cover up your mistakes to make you—and them—seem perfect.

> My parents seem to always be working, coming home to eat and sleep, and then going back out again. Because I never see them, my parents don't know who I am.
> —Sonnet, 15

> My family has set a pretty bad example of respect for my siblings and me. My mom and stepdad had an incredibly nasty divorce and constantly screamed at and about each other. They're definitely not my role models when it comes to what a healthy, loving, respectful adult relationship should be like. —Susana, 17

Respect Rx: If others don't accept you, it hurts—but it doesn't hurt as much if you can learn to accept yourself. Yet, you still need at least *some* validation, right? Communication is the place to start. Tell your family members how you feel when they don't accept you. Those who love you will listen. They may not have realized how their remarks or expectations have hurt you. Another step is to lead by example by accepting your family members for who *they* are.

Your right: To feel like you belong and are an equal.

Your right disrespected: When your parents play favorites by treating your brothers, sisters, stepsiblings, or birth children better than you. When boys in the family have more freedoms than girls, such as being able to date at a younger age or stay out later. When a parent puts you down, either in front of you or behind your back.

Respect Rx: When you're not treated as an equal it *isn't* a reflection of how valuable you are. Don't start to believe you're not worth much and treat yourself that way, too. Instead, talk to your family about the inequalities you see and how you feel about them. Don't be afraid to ask questions like, "Why do some family members have more privileges than others?" Explain that for you to be a strong, successful girl who's not held back in life, your empowerment needs to start at home. If they don't get it or don't respond, make sure to find a supportive person to talk to (see page 86).

Your right: To speak your mind, change your mind, and question the world around you.

Your right disrespected: When your family believes that "Children should be seen and not heard." When your family isn't big on honesty, and you feel like you can't bring up tough topics. When you're simply not allowed to express your own opinions if they differ from those of your family.

Respect Rx: Most girls learn something real fast from their families: Everyone's got an opinion! Some families operate like a freedom-of-speech forum in which everyone constantly talks about their feelings and debates their points. But in other families, what the adults say goes. No matter what your family is like, if there's love in your home, there's room for more Communication 101. You might need to work on your confidence before you start speaking up and questioning what's going on. If certain people in your family don't want to have open, honest communication, talk with other adults (like mentors or teachers) and your friends for support.

Your right: To become independent.

Your right disrespected: When your parents don't let you take healthy risks, give you age-appropriate responsibilities, or allow you much privacy. When you can't solve your own problems because your family always bails you out. When your choice of friends, after-school activities, or clothes is often criticized.

Respect Rx: Show your family that you can handle more independence and that you're prepared to make mistakes and learn from them. If your family criticizes your choices, let them know (respectfully) that their negative comments are hurtful. Despite these obstacles, keep forging your own path!

Your right: To follow your passions and be the real you.

Your right disrespected: When your parents seem to have your entire future mapped out for you—from your extracurricular activities to what you'll be when you grow up. When you're not allowed to pursue your interests, or you have to pretend to be someone you're not to get along.

Respect Rx: Instead of getting frustrated, get curious. Ask the adults in your family how they came up with their plans for you. Next step: negotiation. Ask if you can try *one* new activity—something you're really passionate about. Set a goal and ask your mom or dad to support you in reaching it. If your family sees you doing something that makes you proud, there's a good chance they'll be proud of you, too.

Your right: To listen to your true feelings.

Your right disrespected: When a family member manipulates you to go against your boundaries (threatening to withhold love, making you feel guilty, or giving you disapproving looks). When you're told to ignore your feelings ("You're *so* sensitive," "Stop being a baby," or "Grow up"). When you know in your gut that something is wrong—such as when a family member lies or is abusive—but you ignore it because you don't want to cause trouble.

Respect Rx: Trusting your feelings and gut instincts is a must for any self-respecting girl. You can tell your family how you feel when they don't listen to you or respect you. Another option is to filter the comments your family makes, instead of taking them to heart. But don't ignore it if something harmful is going down in your family (emotional abuse, for example). Get some help from a relative or a trusted adult outside of your family.

Your right: To figure out what you need and take care of yourself.

Your right disrespected: When it feels like no one is on your side. When a parent isn't there for you emotionally (due to divorce, drug or alcohol addiction, imprisonment, or other issues). When your family environment isn't healthy, for whatever reason, including not meeting your basic needs for food, clothing, and medical care.

Respect Rx: Your needs are important. If you can't meet some of them yourself, then ask for more family support. Maybe a relative, clergy member, or close family friend can provide some help. Don't give up until you find an adult who's willing to listen and get involved.

Sometimes, parents who are depressed or who abuse alcohol or drugs are neglectful or abusive, or may abandon their children. If you're in this situation, it doesn't mean that your parents don't love you. Even though you love them, it's not your job to fix them. As difficult as it is to watch them hurt themselves, you can't change them—they have to *want* to get help. Talk to a school counselor or another trusted adult for advice. On pages 204–205, you'll find a list of helplines you can call 24/7 for support.

Your right: To feel and be safe.

Your right disrespected: When your family members call you names or put you down in other ways. When they hit or physically hurt you (or abuse you sexually). When family adults are in abusive relationships (they fight all the time, or one of them hits the other). When a parent has such serious problems that the whole family is at risk, such as being exposed to crime, drug abuse, weapons, or violence.

Respect Rx: All of these situations are abusive (see Chapter 9 to learn about abuse and where to turn for help). If this is going on in your home, you probably feel unprotected, stressed out, and scared most of the time. And you might also feel like you don't deserve respect or love—even from yourself (but you do!). If you're being abused in any way, seek help immediately from a trusted adult, a support group, or a legal or social service agency. In your heart, always know that you have a right to get the support you need and to feel safe.

Standing By Your SIBS

Siblings: You love them (most of the time), you need them, and you usually have no choice but to live with them. As close as you are to them, they may be the people who most get on your nerves. Your sibs might be your best friends or seem like they come from a totally different family (and maybe they do if they're stepsiblings or half siblings). No matter how you get along now, your sibs are yours—they're going to be in your life. When it comes to your brothers and sisters, standing by them is essential.

Do you and your sibs act more like rivals than friends? If you ignore each other's rights, yell at each other all the time, or even hurt each other physically, disrespect has taken over. Talk with your sisters and brothers about the arguments and how you'd like your relationship to change. You can grow closer if you stick together, instead of playing the competition game or fighting for a parent's attention.

Be an example by showing your sibs some respect, even at times when they're not doing the same. You can help keep the peace by being more supportive and by using many of the tips in "Communication 101" (page 70). At first, your sibs might not respond with a smile and a hug—it may take time for them to adjust to a new way of relating to you. Don't give up.

> My older sister is my cheerleader. She says, "You can do this. You can make it through." She's always there to listen to me and offer advice.
> —Keisha, 16

SISTERHOOD

If you've got sisters, you have the opportunity for a really special relationship. Sisters can be your confidantes, mentors, and friends. In fact, you can begin to build sisterhood among all the girls in your life by starting at home with your *real* sisters. Start now, under your roof, by respecting your sisters and helping each other fine-tune your family's communication skills. Girls are more powerful when they work together to spread respect!

At times, you may need to set boundaries with your sibs (and vice versa). Check out these scenarios, which can inspire you to speak up without letting a conflict heat up:

~~~~~~

Your sister: Borrows your clothes without asking and doesn't give them back. Or she returns them with stains or holes.

Try: "I feel _____ when you take my stuff and then return it all messed up. I respect you, and that's why I don't take your clothes without asking. Please ask me before you borrow my clothes. Otherwise, I won't be able to trust you, and I really want to."

~~~~~~

Your brother: Makes fun of you, tells you what to do, or puts you down if you don't do things his way.

Try: "When you boss me around or put down my choices, I feel _____. You're really smart and know a lot, but I have to be my own person. Instead of telling me what to do, please wait for me to ask for your advice. And when you don't agree with my choices, please don't be so critical. It makes me feel _____."

~~~~~~

Your sister: Manipulates your parents to get out of chores—or doesn't have many—and you often do her share of the work.

Try: "When you get out of your chores, I have to do them, and I feel _____. How would you feel in my place? We have to treat each other like equals—no matter what our parents do—to respect each other."

~~~~~~

Your brother: Snoops in your room, listens in on phone calls, or reads your email.

Try: "I feel _____ when you get into my personal business. I respect your privacy, so please respect mine. If you want to know more about me, just ask. I'll be honest if I feel comfortable telling you stuff. But we need more trust between us first, and that means no more spying."

~~~~~~

Your sister: Yells at you, calls you names, or hits you.

Try: "When you do that, I feel _____. You have no right to hurt or disrespect me. This has to stop today. Don't take stuff out on me anymore. I care about you, and I want us to have a better relationship."

Sibling Pact

It might seem touchy-feely to make a pact with your sibs, but it's a whole lot better than fighting.

You can use this one as a model or create your own.

We promise that we will . . .

- listen to each other

- not bully or manipulate each other

- avoid put-downs, criticism, and arguments

- not compete for love or attention

- honor each other's boundaries

- encourage and stand up for each other

- apologize when we've hurt each other

- love each other just the way we are

Signed: _____

Signed: _____

Date: _____

Finding SUPPORTIVE Adults

Parents sometimes have issues or make choices that mean they're not in your life like they should be. Maybe they work all the time. Maybe they have health problems or live far away. Sometimes, parents have emotional issues and don't know how to make changes so they *can* be closer to you. There may be other reasons why a parent isn't around: You could be in foster care, placed for adoption, or moving around between relatives.

When a caring parent isn't available, you can look outside of your family for support. Adult role models—or mentors—can provide the guidance and inspiration you need. Mentors are trusted adults who listen to your concerns or feelings, offer you a new perspective, and help you reach your goals in life. Even if your relationships with family adults are strong, you could still benefit from a mentor who helps you build your skills and your self-respect.

Here's what to look for in a mentor:

A strong woman. It's important for any girl to have a confident, self-respecting woman as a mentor. Men can make great mentors, too, but a woman has gone through something that no man has: being a teen girl. Your mentor could be a family member, like an aunt, or she could be a family friend, teacher, or volunteer with an organization for girls.

Support. Above all, mentors should be sources of encouragement. They can help you find new challenges and learn from mistakes. They can offer advice or guide you when you're trying to solve a problem. Your mentor should be someone you look up to—and someone you can count on while remaining true to yourself.

Safety. Finding a mentor through adults you already know and trust is a smart idea. You can probably get a mentor through your school, place of worship, or community center. Or try a national organization that screens and trains mentors, such as Big Brothers Big Sisters, Boys and Girls Clubs, the YMCA, or the YWCA.

Try these tips to help you and your mentor get to know each other better and stay close:

Break the ice. Think of something you have in common or that interests you about her and bring it up. Ask a question like, "Why did you become a mentor?" or "How did you get your job doing _____?"

Get talking. Once you get to know your mentor a bit better, tell her what you hope to get out of the relationship. Do you want her to teach you a certain skill or be your support system when you try something new?

Respect her boundaries. Your mentor is a friend and someone you should respect. So, be on time and be prepared for your meetings. Find out if she has preferences about calling her at home or at work, or if it's OK to email her. Listen when she talks, ask her questions, and show that you're interested in her life, too.

Be appreciative. Send your mentor thank-you cards and little tokens of your appreciation when possible. Keep her posted on your accomplishments or invite her to your celebrations, like graduations, award ceremonies, or other special events where you're showing your stuff.

And, by the way, you don't have to stop at just one mentor—some girls have several or even a long list of them. Most important, choose mentors who will inspire you and believe in you (you're worth the investment!).

FRIENDS 'TIL THE END ...

Girls say they need good friends like they need food and water—friends are necessary for survival. We asked girls how they support their friends and how they want to be treated in return, and their answers all pointed to respect:

When something bad happens, my friends are always there for me, and when something good happens, they share in my happiness.—Robin, 15

I can't trust anyone in my family, so I turn to my friends for support.—April, 14

In a true friendship, you respect each other and treat each other kindly. —Alexia, 15

Around my friends in my Girl Scout troop, I am myself. They know who I am and that I like to act goofy and have fun.—Jenna, 15

When I figured out who I really was, I found a group of friends who respect the real me.—Olivia, 16

I always feel like I can be real around my friends because I know that they won't judge me.—Marissa, 15

6

Friends

Friends are there for you when you need them and a blast to be around when you want to have fun. They can become your secret-keepers, your #1 support network, and your most important sounding board. Good friends start to become like your family (a family you get to choose).

You may not have thought about it, but your friends are a reflection of how you see yourself. When your self-respect is low, you might hang out with friends who don't care much about themselves, bring you down, or hold you back. But when your self-respect is booming, you're more likely to surround yourself with friends who like you the way you are, quirks and all. When you have good friends, you also learn to be a better friend to someone who really matters: you.

SISTERhood

It's a respect basic: building strong relationships. This includes forming solid bonds with other girls or, put another way, joining the sisterhood. Being a part of the sisterhood is about feeling like you're connected with all females in the world and caring about their rights. It starts at home by boosting respect among the girlfriends you already have and branching out from there.

Sisterhood can inspire you to be the best person you can be—because you have friends who stick by you through all the ups and downs and in between. And why do they? Because your girlfriends probably get what you're dealing with every day—they're going through it, too. When you have sisterhood in your life, you have a greater sense of belonging and safety. You have power because you can stand by, and for, other girls. You have wisdom because you're learning from other girls, instead of competing with them. And you enjoy more of your rights because you can work together to ensure that every girl can be herself without limitations.

The cool thing is that the girlfriends you have now might be with you for life. They could be your first hires when you make it to the White House, or the only people who will always be able to make you bust out laughing with a single word or sly look. Even if the friends you have now aren't your best friends forever, you can learn a lot from them. They can teach you how to be a good friend and what to look for in your future friendships.

When you appreciate your girlfriends just the way they are, it helps you appreciate yourself just the way *you* are. And that's why it's important for sisterhood to be a part of your life, today and forever. Here are some ways to make it last:

Be Yourself

When you're around your friends, you've got to feel totally free, like you can do or say almost anything and still be accepted. You should be able to be honest about your feelings, goals, and experiences because you know that what you say will be heard and kept private. The bottom line: With your true friends, you can be the true you.

How you treat each other will let you know if trust and closeness are growing (or not). Do you want to see each other stretching to new heights? Do you help each other make smart, healthy choices? Do you cheer each other on and compliment each other on special talents, abilities, and accomplishments? If not, you can take the lead in making your friendships stronger. You can set an example by not competing with your friends or crossing their boundaries. Respect them for being the unique individuals they are—and they should respect you in return.

Friends Like Me

What do your friendships say about how you feel about yourself? Take a close look at what you think you deserve:

The kind of people I admire and want to be around include: _____

My friends treat other people like:_____

My friendships make my life better (or worse) because:_____

My friends treat themselves with respect/disrespect in the following ways:_____

I am a good friend because:_____

My choice of friends says that I am:_____

Be Caring

When you and your friends talk—whether you're chatting on the phone or sharing something personal—you should feel supported (and vice versa). A true friend tries to understand when you're going through changes and challenges. And when you make a mistake, a true friend stands by you and encourages you to do better next time. That's just Friendship 101.

Here's a rule to live by: Friends stick up for each other when they're together *and* when they're apart. Do you and your friends follow this rule? Do you show your friends you care by listening to their problems and keeping their confidences? Do you try not to gossip about each other? And what happens when you disagree—do you work through it and forgive each other? Putting these basics into place will strengthen the bonds of sisterhood.

Bound-a-ries, Please

If you ever need to vent about a situation you're having with one friend, don't go to someone else in your circle of friends. Why? Because what you say might get back to her, and she could feel hurt and betrayed. Instead, vent to someone who doesn't hang out with her, like your mom, your aunt, or a friend from another school.

Be Honest

You have to know what you feel comfortable with before you let it all hang out with your friends. That's because trust is at the core of any relationship. But do you know who you can trust? Do your friends listen to you without judging you (and do you do the same)? Do you always have each other's best interests at heart?

As with your other relationships, you can be honest and set boundaries in your friendships. To do this, tell the truth about your feelings. For example, if you don't want to talk about something personal or if a friend's teasing has hurt you, speak up. Good girlfriends don't walk all over each other's boundaries or get offended by them. Remember: Boundaries can actually help you grow closer and build more respect.

If your friends pressure you and you feel uncomfortable, it's time for a gut check. Ask yourself what you want and why. Are your friends really on your side? Are they honoring your rights? Don't go against your boundaries and gut checks just to please your friends. (For tips on how to stand up to a friend, go to "Disrespect Dilemmas" on page 94.) And if *you're* the one pushing your friends to ignore *their* boundaries, be truthful with yourself: Why are you doing it? Do you like to feel more powerful than your friends? Are you insecure about your choices?

Be Invested

Your friends are there for you—so be there for them. Try not to take them for granted. Even though your life is probably busy, remember to show your girlfriends that you're interested in their lives. If a friend is in a school play, be there on opening night. Or if she has a difficult paper to write, tell her she can call you if she gets stuck. Whenever you can, be there for them if your friends have a problem and need your support.

You might have heard this one before, but it's solid advice: Don't let a crush come between you and a friend, or drop your friends the minute you get into a romantic relationship. Most teen loves don't last forever, but your friendships can. If you make your friendships a priority, then you'll still have someone who cares about you long after your first relationships or breakups. When you're there for your girlfriends, they'll feel valued and you'll see the payoff: Good friendships make your life rich!

Speak Up

What about those times when your friends seem to take *you* for granted? You probably feel hurt and ignored—and those feelings can quickly turn to anger. Before this happens, speak up and tell your friend you need her. Try, "I've missed you lately—what's going on? Can we start spending more time together again?"

Be Open to New Friends

You might be lucky enough to have friendships that go way back to when you were a little girl. On the other hand, you may have moved or changed schools, which meant making new friends along the way. If you don't have someone you consider a best friend, think about whether you've got close friends—people you like a lot and feel comfortable being around.

Your friends can come from all walks of life. In fact, when you make friends with people who aren't exactly like you (including guys), chances are you'll learn more about yourself, others, and the world. Best-friend status doesn't develop overnight, but you can get to that point by spending lots of time together, talking, and meeting each other's family and other friends.

Sometimes, friendships at school can be loaded with past baggage. Maybe you had a not-so-glorious moment in sixth grade that none of your friends will let you live down, and it feels like the rest of your school career is forever ruined. Want a fresh start? Surround yourself with supportive girls outside of school by joining a girl-centric organization in your area that helps girls become stronger and more confident.

Most of these groups were actually started to help girls become more powerful—so you'll have found the right place to build your self-respect. You can have fun, work together to make a difference, or just meet new friends. Plus, you'll get to know some cool women who mentor or coach these groups and can inspire you now and for the rest of your life.

Sisterhood Pact

You and your friend(s) can support each other by making a pact. Get together and list the ways you'll respect yourselves and your friendship, and then sign a pledge to always support each other. Through the years, hold onto your pact and when times get tough, pull it out as a reminder of the promise you've made.

We promise that we will . . .

❧ respect ourselves, body, mind, and heart

❧ follow our passions and interests

❧ keep our relationship strong

❧ honor each other's boundaries

❧ encourage and support each other always

❧ be a part of the sisterhood

Signed: _____

Signed: _____

Date: _____

Disrespect DILEMMAS

All friendships have rough spots. There will be times when you misunderstand each other and need to check in. Don't be afraid of conflicts—they can actually make your friendship stronger if you're both willing to work things out. If you don't talk about issues or misunderstandings, you risk growing apart.

There are certain rules when it comes to talking to your friends about your feelings and needs. Keep these respect rules in mind, so you say what you mean instead of something you'll regret:

Rule #1: Think ahead of time about what you're going to say. What's bothering you? What happened? How did it make you feel? What might make things better? If you're nervous, writing down your thoughts and rehearsing what you'll say could help.

Rule #2: Don't confront your friend in front of other people. Find a place that feels safe and private. Ask your friend if she can meet you there to talk, instead of confronting her when she least expects it. (See #9 for an exception to this rule.)

Rule #3: Focus on sharing how you feel (not on everything your friend has done wrong), so she's more likely to hear you out. Try, "I feel really hurt when you tease me in front of other people, even if you think you're just joking around."

Rule #4: Avoid phrases that could put your friend on the defensive like, "You always _____," or "You never _____." Instead, be specific about what's bothering you and what you want to change. Try, "I feel _____ when you criticize my appearance. I'd feel better if you'd stop."

Rule #5: If your friend gets defensive, ask her if she'd like more time to think about what you've said. Offer to call her later or to meet up with her again when she's more open to what you have to say.

Rule #6: Try to stay calm and express how you feel using carefully chosen words. If your feelings overwhelm you and you start to cry, just say you need a minute to calm down or ask her if you can talk again later.

Rule #7: Be assertive, which means using a strong, serious voice (without yelling) and making eye contact. And pay attention to your body language. If you stand with your arms crossed, you may look aggressive. But if you look down the whole time you're talking, your friend might not realize that you mean what you say.

Rule #8: Expect her to pay attention and take you seriously. If your friend tries to make light of your concerns or won't look at you, try, "I feel like you're not paying attention to me. Should we talk another time?"

Rule #9: If your friend has intimidated you in the past, you might feel more confident if you have a mutual friend close by for support. Your supporter can stand near you or within earshot, so she can step in if the conversation gets out of control. Be up front about why your other friend is standing by you: "We're not ganging up on you—I just wanted her here for support and because she knows us both so well."

Rule #10: End the conversation in a way you both feel good about. If your friend says she's sorry, accept her apology gracefully. Thank her for listening. Let her know that you're really glad to have her as a friend.

WHEN FRIENDS AREN'T SO FRIENDLY

I've been in verbally and physically abusive friendships with girls. For a while, they were really wearing me down, but I've found a way to tell them it's not OK to talk to me like that or hit me.—Bianca, 15

Disrespect in a friendship is breaking trust, backstabbing, spreading rumors, putting a friend down in front of others, and not standing up for a friend.—Leah, 16

I had a "friend" in seventh grade who basically ruled our group of friends by terrorizing us. I was always afraid that she was going to make fun of me, or hit or push me—and then say, "Just kidding."—Andie, 14

I don't need friends who make themselves feel better by hurting me or cutting me down.—Britney, 14

Friendship Rx

Every friendship is unique, but some of the same issues seem to come up for many girls. Here's how to deal with common dilemmas by speaking up and setting boundaries:

Dilemma: A friend is critical of everything you do.

The respect connection: Supportive feedback can help you grow into a better person. But if your friend doesn't let you be yourself—criticizing everything from what you wear to what you say—she's going overboard. Pulitzer Prize-winning writer Jules Feiffer calls these biting remarks "Little Murders." And they are: of your self-respect.

Rx: First, don't take everything your friend says as fact. Her comments are probably more about *her* than about you. Let your friend know how she's hurting you by saying something like, "I feel really bad when you cut me down. Maybe you don't mean to sound harsh, but it still hurts. I need you to be more supportive of me."

Dilemma: A friend pressures you to do things you don't want to do, and then lays a guilt trip on you if you refuse.

The respect connection: Your friend isn't listening to your boundaries, and she's stepping on your rights.

Rx: Set your boundary again in a firm voice, saying, "I told you that I don't want to do _____. Please respect my reasons, even if you don't agree with them." You could add, "You're not going to change my mind by making me feel guilty. Please don't pressure me this way."

Dilemma: You tell your friend something private, and she tells your other friends.

The respect connection: Gossip isn't a friendly pastime—it poisons friendships. Betrayals like this can hurt you to the core and, if they happen, you've got to decide how to speak up and stay strong.

Rx: At first, withhold judgment and get the story straight. It could have been an honest mistake (like your friend accidentally let your secret slip), so bring it up with her when she's alone. If she admits to talking behind your back, then you can remind her why she needs to keep your business private—and you can ask for an apology.

Dilemma: Some of your friends gang up on other friends in your group, including you.

The respect connection: In a true friendship, there can't be a "queen bee" and a "wannabe" (a leader and a follower). In a group of friends, one girl might be more outspoken and play the role of organizer, but there shouldn't be an undertone of "I'm the boss" or "You'd better listen to me or you're out." In supportive friendships, girls don't use bullying or manipulation to get what they want or have control. Sisterhood means genuinely caring about each other and letting each girl have a voice.

Rx: The next time your friends gang up on you, don't ignore it until it blows over. Tell them something like, "I feel like you're all turning on me. It hurts my feelings and makes me wonder if you're my true friends. Why are you doing this?" If they start a campaign against another friend, stand up on her behalf. Try, "I don't want to play that game. I like her, and I'm not going to do that to her. We're supposed to be friends, not enemies."

Dilemma: A friend asks to copy your homework, borrows money without paying you back, or only comes around for access to your stuff or other people in your life.

The respect connection: Your friend is using you, and that's disrespectful. The friends you choose should like you for *you,* not what you can do for them. If you find yourself trying to "buy" a friend's attention or acceptance, you're not seeing your own value. You're worth more than that!

Rx: Talk to your friend about how you feel. And set a boundary like, "I keep lending you my stuff, but you haven't returned anything. Before you borrow something else, I'd like my things back." Then follow through. If she's a real friend, she'll get the message and change her ways.

Dilemma: Your friend talks about herself all the time.

The respect connection: Respectful communication requires give and take—you both need to be equally interested in each other and to be heard.

Rx: Your friend might not know that she's being "me, me, me" most of the time. Gently point out that you feel like she doesn't listen to you. Tell her that it would mean a lot to you if she'd ask you more questions and let you talk. If she's your true friend, she'll probably work on it.

Dilemma: You have a friend who's totally moody, and you have to be careful about what you do or say when you're around her.

The respect connection: It's possible that your friend's mood swings are caused by a mental-health problem, or that she's having trouble at home. But in a case like this, you also have to listen to your gut. If your friend lashes out at you all the time, that doesn't sound like friendship. Her moodiness could be a form of bullying if she intimidates you on purpose.

Rx: Ask your friend if she needs your help. You could recommend that she seek support by giving her the number of a peer-counseling helpline or asking an adult to help. If you can't find an explanation for your friend's behavior and she continues to treat you poorly, you can start putting a little distance between the two of you by spending more time with other friends.

Dilemma: A friend is nice to you when the two of you hang out, but she treats you like she barely knows you when others are around.

The respect connection: True friends don't change how they feel about you depending on the situation or who's around. A friend should always stand by you—and you should always do the same for her. That's what sisterhood is all about.

Rx: Tell your friend why her behavior is disrespectful. Try, "When we're alone, we're really close and have fun together. But when we're with other people, it's like you ignore me or you pretend we're not even friends. If we're going to stay friends, we need to treat each other with respect *always.*"

Saying GOOD-BYE

After reading the respect dilemmas, you might think, "Yeah, right. If I stood up for myself that way, I'd lose all my friends!" But think about it. If you can't flex your self-respect around your friends, what kind of friends are you hanging out with?

Here's the deal: You can't truly respect yourself if your relationships leave you feeling stressed out or left out. Sometimes, the people you were friends with when you were younger start to go in a direction that you don't want for yourself—like getting into trouble or making choices you think are harmful. Or maybe you and some of your friends no longer have the same interests, so you don't feel like hanging out with them as much. What do you do when certain friendships have run their course? For starters, you can seek out new friends who will support you and help pump up your self-respect.

There may be times when you feel it's best to end a friendship, like when you don't feel supported. It's never easy to end a friendship, especially if you know you'll still see the person every day at school. The goal is to end the relationship considerately so there aren't too many hard feelings.

Before ending the relationship or phasing out a friend, make sure that you:

Give it some thought. Spend time writing in your journal. Be honest with yourself about why the friendship may be beyond repair. Consider whether you want to officially "break up" with your friend, or if you'd prefer to start spending more time with new people until the old friendship is phased out.

Get ready. When relationships change, feelings can get hurt. Your friend might be angry with you when you tell her that the friendship needs to end. She might even try to turn your other friends against you. For a while, you'll probably be anxious or you might feel guilty. Write in your journal about the possible outcomes. What do you hope will happen? How might your friend react? Putting your thoughts on paper can help you feel more prepared. Talk to your mom or another adult (like the school counselor) and get some advice on handling the situation respectfully.

Make other friends. If you think that ending the friendship may cause other friends to break up with you in return, start making new friends now so you'll have more support. Hang out with other people you get along with. Join a club or sports team at school, so you can meet potential friends. Ask other girls (or guys) if they want to hang out at lunch or do something after school or on the weekend. Start spending more time at your local community center or in other places where lots of girls gather for group activities and events. If you belong to a place of worship, consider joining its youth group. Don't be afraid to put yourself out there!

Practice. Ask someone you trust to help you rehearse what you'll say to your friend. You could even role-play the conversation with a family member.

Be strong. While it's tempting to send an email or write a note, you should talk to your friend in person. She deserves a face-to-face conversation.

You can use the following ideas to help break the news gently.

How to start:

"We've been friends for a while, and we've been through a bunch of fun and serious times. It's hard to say this, but . . ." (and then continue with one of the options below, depending on what's true for you).

Next say:

". . . I feel like we've grown apart, so I'm going to hang out with people I have more in common with."

". . . I need to feel like my friends accept and respect me and my feelings. I'm not getting that in my friendship with you."

". . . I feel like I'm trying to be someone I'm not in order to stay friends with you, but I don't want to keep doing that. It's time for me to move on and find other friends."

Often, you'll discover that you *both* actually feel the same way about the friendship needing to end. (And you'll probably both give a huge sigh of relief.) On the other hand, your friend might get upset, get angry, or cry. Offer what comfort you can and try to find a way to exit gracefully (the tips that follow might help).

Wrap it up:

"I'm sorry things ended up this way, but I hope you know our friendship has been important to me."

"I hope we can stay friendly with each other, instead of being mad or hurt."

If your friend wants to talk about it more, give her the chance. She might need feedback from you to work through her feelings or to grow from the experience. But if at any point she crosses your boundaries, you can end the conversation and explain why you're doing so.

Give yourself some time to deal with the anger, sadness, or guilt that may come with the loss of a close friendship. Talk to your other friends or write in your journal about your feelings.

Friendship Film Festival

Watching movies is a great way to take a look at friendships from the outside. Choose one or two movies and get together with your girlfriends to critique how the friendships are portrayed. You'll probably notice girl/girl and girl/guy relationships that are respectful, disrespectful, or a bit of both, which is usually the case in real life. Consider these questions as you watch each flick:

❧ In what ways do the friends show sisterhood? In what ways do the friends respect each other (or not)?

❧ Did a friend have to change who she was to be accepted by the group? Why?

❧ What did the friends value about each other? How did they show it?

❧ Overall, were the friendships respectful or disrespectful? How so?

As a bonus, you might combine this movie night with "Throw a Media Critic Party" (see page 64) to call out any negative ways that girls are stereotyped in the films.

reTroSPECT:
equal (relationship) rights

Lucretia Mott and Elizabeth Cady Stanton organized the first U.S. women's convention in Seneca Falls, New York, in July 1848. Though only 300 people showed up, the meeting planted the seed for the groundbreaking women's rights movement of the next century. The supporters signed the Declaration of Sentiments, a list of rights for women that called for them to be able to freely speak their minds, to earn their own money, to own property—and not be owned by their husbands. The Declaration stated the facts of the day: *"Mankind has endeavored, in every way that he could, to destroy [a woman's] confidence in her own powers, to lessen her self-respect, and to make her willing to lead a dependent . . . life. We hold these truths to be self-evident: that all men and women are created equal."*[1] And that was just the beginning!

Your rights are so much stronger today, thanks to these early crusaders and those who are still working on behalf of girls and women everywhere. You have the right to be an equal and to decide on your own relationship rules and readiness. You have the right to say no, to be safe, and to end a relationship that's disrespectful. Some of these rights are the law, while others you have to personally stand up for each day. Defining your relationship rights—and making them happen—is up to you.

7

Relationships

The term "relationship," in the romantic sense, means different things to different girls. A relationship can mean hanging out, dating, or hooking up. It can mean being in love or being in "like a lot." Put simply, a relationship typically involves two people who are admittedly more than friends (secret crushes don't count).

Depending on what you know or are discovering about yourself, you can be in a relationship with a boy, girl, or both. (To keep it simple, we'll refer to your like or love interests as boyfriend/girlfriend, or BF/GF.) Based on your boundaries and choices, your relationships might involve physical intimacy, like holding hands, hugging, kissing, cuddling, touching, or sexual activity.

Getting to know people, getting intimate, or giving a part of your heart can feel amazing, like there are hundreds of butterflies fluttering around inside you. At one point or another, most people want to be loved and to give love in return. Many girls explore love through BF/GF relationships, while others choose to reserve their loving feelings for their family, friends, sense of spirituality, or even their pets. It just depends on where your heart leads you and what you're ready for.

Respect is a big part of any romantic relationship. When you don't have respect, it's impossible for the relationship to be healthy. For example, how can you feel good if a BF/GF is mean to you or ignores you? How can you say what's on your mind if you're not being heard or you don't have trust? How can you know what you're ready for when it comes to physical intimacy if you don't respect yourself or your BF/GF? And how can you be sure that the relationship is the real thing if you don't think your BF/GF likes the real you? *You* are the one who decides whether or not to start (and stick with) a relationship. Never forget that.

> You can't put too much energy and time into getting a boyfriend or girlfriend. All that energy should be put into yourself so you can grow, better yourself, and have a powerful effect on the world.
> —Rashida, 16

The Three MAGIC Words

Some girls think that relationships start with a chase—looking good and catching the eye of a crush—and then falling madly in love. The giddy feeling you get in the beginning of a new relationship is great, but it doesn't last forever. So, where does attraction end and respect begin? It's about more than saying, "I love you." You have to be able to say (and mean) these three-word promises, too: *I like you. I trust you. I respect you.*

> It's OK to have a boyfriend or girlfriend, but when you need to be in a relationship to feel good about yourself, you're not respecting yourself.
> —Sonja, 14

 ## I Like You + You Like Me

When you truly like people, you admire them for more than their looks or popularity. You see who they are on the *inside:* what they stand for and believe in, what they want in life, and who they want to be. Liking someone shouldn't be confused with infatuation, which is a fleeting passion or obsession for a person you hardly know.

When someone likes you for you (and vice versa), then you have the beginnings of a great relationship. And that means you don't try to change or control each other. Instead, you care for each other's well-being. This is what makes it possible for your hearts to grow closer, for you to support each other in your own pursuits, and for trust to grow.

 ## I Trust You + You Trust Me

What makes a relationship really special? It isn't red roses on Valentine's Day. It's trust—the kind that allows you to feel free to be yourself in a relationship and to know that your heart, mind, and body will be respected.

Trust has to go both ways, and it starts with being honest. You honor the trust you've been given by being truthful or admitting when you've lied. With a trust that's real (and allows for mistakes), you and your BF/GF will be able to talk openly about what you want and how you feel. You should both be able to define the terms of the relationship, like whether

> In a good relationship, you both communicate clearly about how you're feeling, and you're both faithful to each other and truthful with each other about everything.
> —Maydeline, 16

you're exclusive or dating other people—or be honest about whether the relationship needs to end. Trust makes it possible to become closer and is essential if your relationship gets physical (see Chapter 8).

♥ I Respect You + You Respect Me

By now, you know that having self-respect means listening to yourself, setting boundaries, speaking up, and expecting to be treated as an equal. Good relationships rely on those same basics. If you're not respected by a BF/GF, you could start to believe that you're not worthy of being treated well—and that's a major pitfall.

Getting respect in your relationships starts with you. You need to get in touch with what's in your heart before you let someone else stake a claim to it. And remember: You get what you

WHAT MaKeS a reLATIONSHIP THe reaL THING?

It's built on three things: love, trust, and respect.
—Alissa, 14

A guy will treat you the way you allow him to treat you. He won't know the limits unless you set them.—Alicia, 16

When you listen to each other, that's the real thing. When you don't do anything on purpose to hurt each other. When you care about each other's well-being, like paying attention to the people you're hanging out with and whether you're both safe.—Kathryn, 15

A really good relationship is when two people can tell each other anything and not be afraid to tell the other what they are thinking.—Brianna, 14

When you don't pressure each other to do anything in terms of sex, drinking, or other stuff that one of you is even remotely uncomfortable with. Letting each other know that you are important to each other.—Lisa, 17

Both partners have to be equals—love can't exist if equality doesn't exist. You also have to be friends before you become a couple, to communicate openly and frequently, and to be honest with each other about what you want, need, and expect from one another.—Angela, 17

give. If you communicate honestly and care about your BF's/GF's well-being, then you set the tone for how you want to be treated in return.

POP the Questions

What does having a relationship mean to you? What are your standards for a relationship? In other words, what do you want? The answers aren't always obvious and will change as you do. Sometimes, you have to search your mind—and heart— to discover what you're *really* looking for. Remember to keep questioning yourself, so you always know *why* you want a relationship.

Question #1:
Are you relationship-ready?

Ignore what you might have been told in all those fairytales and sappy soaps: You don't *need* a BF/GF to be happy or complete. In fact, putting all your energy into getting and keeping a BF/GF can make you *less* complete—because you may miss out on learning about yourself and exploring your own interests.

You shouldn't be in a relationship just to be accepted.
—Carolee, 16

Before you turn on your supersonic flirting powers, it helps to think about why you want to get together with someone. Are you truly a relationship-ready girl? Or are tons of outside forces nudging—or shoving—you toward feeling like you need a BF/GF? Are you lacking in love at home and hoping to find it somewhere else? How will (or does) being in a relationship make your life better or help you learn more about yourself?

Don't dive headfirst into the hookup pool without thinking about all the reasons you're looking for love. If you're already in a relationship, it's never too late to explore the reasons why you chose to get together. If your relationship is about wanting to be accepted or needing attention, take it slow. You might not be totally ready yet.

Question #2:
What kind of person do you like?

Think about the people you choose to hang out with—what traits do you admire in friends, family, or mentors (and yourself)? Do you want your BF/GF to have those qualities, too?

If you only pay attention to people's outside packaging, it's easy to ignore (or miss) any flaws in their attitude. On the flip side, you could overlook some cool, original people if you assume they're not your type and totally write them off. So, know what character traits matter most to you in a BF/GF, and then make an effort to discover them in others (you could be surprised about who ends up sparking your interest).

Really knowing the kind of person you're into means first knowing yourself. As you grow to know yourself more and more, your standards for the kind of person to have a relationship with will also become clearer. It takes time and, like anyone else, you might (as the saying goes) kiss a few frogs along the way. That's just part of the relationship learning curve.

Question #3:
What are your boundaries?

It's hard to know what you might do in every situation and to always be prepared (besides, life could be boring if everything was predictable). But when it comes to relationships, you can set some boundaries based on what your head, heart, and gut are already telling you about what you want and need.

relationship disrespect

My boyfriend's friends would say mean things to me, and he wouldn't stick up for me. He would just laugh at me with them.—Cassandra, 14

One time, my crush and I walked to his house after school. When we went inside, his dad was sitting right there but my crush never introduced me to him. His dad looked at me like I was just another one of his son's girlfriends. It made me feel like I wasn't that important.—Mariel, 15

My ex-boyfriend broke up with me, and he started going out with this other girl the same day. He also told all his friends that we did sexual stuff that we didn't do, and they believed him.—Lindsay, 13

Think ahead about how you want to be treated and what you won't stand for. Figure out your "deal-breakers"—the disrespectful behaviors that would make you end a relationship (for example, if the person starts using drugs, cheats on you, or pushes you too far about sex). Relationship boundaries are about deciding who you'll be close to and letting someone in (or not).

Heart-TO-Hearts

Based on what you see in the media—or feel when your BF/GF walks into the room—relationships can seem like they're all about physical attraction. That's undeniably part of it. But being in a relationship involves more than feeling a flutter in your stomach. You can't have a strong, respectful relationship unless you have open communication. Here are some communication do's and don'ts to live by:

Do . . .

- Clarify the terms of the relationship (are you exclusive, for example, or is it OK to see other people?).

- Speak up about your needs, including how you want to be treated, your body boundaries, and what happens if you're disrespected.

- Ask BFs/GFs how they feel about your needs and boundaries, and if they can honor them. (If they can't, or won't, consider whether that's a deal-breaker for you.)

- Ask BFs/GFs about their boundaries, and decide if you can honor them.

- Be honest when something's bothering you, instead of ignoring your feelings or waiting to explode.

- Listen to your BF's/GF's needs and try to understand.

Don't . . .

- Expect your BFs/GFs to automatically know what you want—no one is a mind reader.

- Go off when you feel disrespected. Instead, catch your breath, take a moment to get clear on how you feel, and set some boundaries.

- Be afraid to speak up. When you're in a situation that goes against your boundaries or gut checks, say so.

- Create drama just to get attention or love.

- Threaten or manipulate your BFs/GFs into doing something they don't feel comfortable with.

- Use your BFs/GFs for target practice, taking out feelings of anger or insecurity on them.

Relationship Role Models?

The kind of treatment—good or bad—that you accept in a relationship is often based on what you've learned or seen while growing up. Write about your relationship role models in your journal.

The relationship that has influenced me most is: _____

I think this relationship is healthy (or unhealthy) because:_____

Both people communicate with respect (or disrespect) when they:_____

Because of this relationship, I've learned that: _____

Devoted to Drama?

Even when you know your boundaries and have communicated them, someone you've fallen for could still be disrespectful at times. No one's perfect, after all. But if your BF/GF often hurts you or acts like he/she doesn't trust you, take a closer look at what's going on.

> If you don't love yourself, you can't love someone else in a healthy way. If you're not sure about who you are or can't accept yourself, that's going to create problems. You have to feel confident about yourself in a relationship, or you'll be jealous and not trust the person you're with.
> —Marisol, 16

Disrespect can often be disguised as passion-filled relationship drama. When a couple's "got drama," it means they fight all the time or seem to enjoy playing games and pushing each other's buttons. These couples break up and make up as often as the rest of us change clothes. Drama addicts usually play out their scenes in front of an audience (like friends and family). The reality is that drama is tiring and disrespectful—to the couple and their audience.

Sure, BF/GF relationships have their ups and downs just like friendships do. At the heart of it, though, your relationship should be something that helps you feel good. If it doesn't, you've got a decision to make: Is all that drama a deal-breaker, or do you want to give the relationship a second chance?

Take a look at these common dilemmas and think about what you and your BF/GF might do to get back on track:

Dilemma: Your BF/GF doesn't listen to you or seem to care when you're upset, and the two of you talk over each other during disagreements.

The respect connection: In healthy relationships, people listen and show each other consideration. You need to know that your needs and boundaries are being heard (and vice versa). It probably hurts when your BF/GF doesn't listen to you, and it may be a sign that he/she doesn't value you as much as you deserve.

What to say: "I don't like to feel ignored. I need you to listen to me, and I'll do the same for you. If we can't respect each other, we shouldn't be together."

If you're not listening, ask yourself:

- What is my listening style? How can I be a better listener? Do I think of what I want to say when someone else is talking? Do I interrupt or jump to conclusions? Do I tune out?

- How do I expect to be listened to? How can I treat my BF/GF with the same consideration?

Dilemma: You found out that your BF/GF has been seeing someone on the side, even though the two of you promised to be exclusive.

The respect connection: Cheating is a major sign of disrespect. If you've talked about being faithful to each other, breaking that promise is both hurtful and dishonest. If your BF/GF is being a player—and you've both said cheating is a deal-breaker—then that's an abuse of your trust.

What to say: "I know that you've been seeing someone behind my back, which goes against the promises we made to each other. I feel _____. I can't be with someone who breaks my trust and lies to me."

If you're cheating, ask yourself:

- Why would I do something that could so easily hurt my BF/GF?

- Why am I seeking attention outside of my relationship?

- How do I feel about being dishonest and cheating?

- Do I need to break up with my BF/GF, so I can work on being more secure with myself?

- How can I be honest about what I've done?

Dilemma: Your BF/GF lies to you about big and small issues.

The respect connection: Lying is a violation of the trust you're supposed to have between you. In a respectful relationship, you've got to be able to be honest about who you are (imperfections and all) and get the honesty you deserve in return.

What to say: "When you lie to me, it puts a wall between us and breaks down any trust we've built. I can only be in a relationship that's based on honesty."

If you're lying, ask yourself:

- What makes me feel like lying about my past, my feelings, what I'm doing, or where I've been?

- Am I afraid to show my BF/GF the real me? Why?

- What are the lies doing to my relationship and my self-respect?

Dilemma: Your crush only calls you to hook up and ignores you the rest of the time.

The respect connection: When you let yourself be used, it could mean that you don't respect yourself and are seeking unhealthy attention. If someone really cares about you, he/she won't take advantage of you. Even if you once said that hooking up was OK, you still have a right to change your mind and set new boundaries.

What to say: "When you only call me to hook up, I feel totally used. Take me off your booty-call speed dial." Or "I want to be in a *real* relationship with you. If that's what you want, too, let's talk about how we're going to treat each other with respect. If that's not what you want, then I have to stop seeing you."

If you're using someone, ask yourself:

- Why am I getting physical with someone I don't really care about—what need am I trying to fulfill?

- How do I feel about treating someone this way?

- How can I give myself what I need?

Dilemma: Your BF/GF calls you or other girls rude names, makes you feel worthless, and/or tells other people about your private moments.

The respect connection: No matter what the reason behind these behaviors, if your BF/GF makes you feel like dirt, you need to put a stop to the disrespect. Even if you're physically attracted to your BF/GF, it's probably time to call it quits—because you deserve better.

What to say: "I respect myself too much to take this."

If you're putting down your BF/GF, ask yourself:

- What does my behavior say about how I feel about myself?

- Why do I take out my anger or insecurities on him/her—what's really bothering me?

- Have I learned abusive behaviors from my family or friends?

- What do I need to change here?

Dilemma: You and your BF/GF get into yelling-at-the-top-of-your-lungs fights or dramatically break up and make up every week.

The respect connection: Sometimes, people get addicted to relationship drama (especially the adrenaline surge of breaking up and making up). Other times, they're just totally confused about what being in a relationship means. Save that kind of drama for primetime and instead put your energy into getting along. If you can't, then consider whether the relationship is healthy. (Tip: It's probably not!)

What to say: "I feel like our arguments are out of control. We need to change how we treat each other. Maybe our breakup should be permanent, unless we can really find a way to work this out."

If you're yelling instead of talking, ask yourself:

- Why is all this conflict happening? What do we get out of it?

- What boundaries do both of us need to put in place?

- Do I want to stay with my BF/GF—is this relationship worth saving?

Dilemma: Your BF/GF can't stand it when you talk to other guys/girls and keeps storming off in a jealous fit.

The respect connection: Jealousy is often connected to insecurity and self-doubt. Everyone gets a *little* jealous at times—but if your BF/GF acts irrational and wants to keep tabs on you at all times, then the relationship is unhealthy. You need to be able to trust each other, and to give each other the space to be yourselves and have other friends. Sometimes, jealousy is actually a part of a cycle of violence in which one partner emotionally, physically, or sexually abuses the other. (See Chapter 9 for help.)

 If your BF/GF is controlling your life, often speaks harshly to you, tries to isolate you, or has physically harmed you in the past (including sexual assault), you are being abused. Go to Chapter 9 to learn more about all forms of abuse or see pages 204–204 for anonymous helplines you can call right now. If you feel like you're in immediate danger, please reach out to a trusted adult for help.

What to say: "I do have other friends—both guys and girls—that I enjoy spending time with. I need you to respect my other relationships because they're important to me."

If you're feeling jealous, ask yourself:

- Why do I get jealous—am I trying to create drama on purpose?

- How do I feel about myself when I get jealous? And afterward?

- Are my feelings legitimate—is he/she betraying me? And if so, why am I staying with this person?

- Am I being abusive?

BREAKING Up

Even the closest relationships can come to an end. There are lots of different reasons why relationships don't last forever (or even for a few weeks or months). People grow apart. They move on or move away. They want different things. They fall for someone else. Or maybe they realize they weren't ready for a relationship in the first place.

A breakup could feel like the worst day of your life—it is a loss—whether you're the one who's calling it off or the one who's getting dumped. Dealing with a painful breakup can even affect other areas of your life, including your relationships with family and friends, your schoolwork, and your activities outside of school. Although you may feel like crawling into a hole and crying your eyes out for a month, it's not the time to be completely alone. Call a friend, spill your heart out to your mom, or talk to someone else you trust.

After you've had a good first cry over your heartache, surround yourself with people you care about and who care about you. It helps to keep busy each day, so you don't sink too far into sad or angry feelings. Staying active helps clear your mind, makes you feel good, and can fend off depression.

A lot of people will probably tell you that the pain won't last forever—and it's true. But when you're dealing with that pain, it can be hard to imagine that you'll ever feel better. Down the road, when some of the heartache has gone away, you may even feel relieved that you're not with your BF/GF anymore.

Ending It

Breaking up with someone can be the ultimate sign of self-respect because you're being honest that a situation isn't right for you and choosing to move on. You might feel like breaking up if you're:

- more sad than happy when you're together

- not having fun together

- frustrated because your BF/GF won't work through problems with you

- worried that the relationship is getting too serious or going too fast

- unable to be yourself

- feeling like you want to spend more time by yourself or with friends

- finding that your rights or boundaries are being disrespected

Here's a two-step plan of action:

#1 Decide. In your journal, list all of your needs that aren't being met in the relationship or why you want to break up. Decide if you're making the best decision for yourself—write about your feelings or talk about them with a friend.

#2 Practice what you'll say. In a breakup situation, you don't have to go into everything that went wrong or place blame. Instead, focus on why you need to get out of the relationship and why it's better for both of you in the long run.

Here are some examples of how the breakup might go.

How to start:

"We've been together for _____, and we've been through a lot. It's hard to say this, but . . ." (and then continue with one of the options below, depending on what's true for you).

Next say:

". . . I feel like we've grown apart. I want to feel close, but it's not possible with us anymore and I need to break up with you."

". . . I need to feel like my BF/GF accepts and respects me and my feelings. I'm not getting that in my relationship with you."

". . . I feel like I'm trying to be someone I'm not and doing things I don't want to do in order to stay together with you. I have to stop doing this, so I need to break up with you."

". . . I'm sorry, but my feelings for you have changed. I don't feel the way I used to, and I can't be in this relationship anymore."

Wrap it up:

Sometimes, you'll discover that you *both* feel the same way about why the relationship needs to end. On the other hand, your BF/GF might get really upset. If this happens, don't pass judgment on his/her feelings. Instead, offer some comfort. You might say, "I can see you feel _____. Do you need some time alone?"

Maybe you want to stay friends after the breakup, or maybe you don't. It's not a rule that you have to stay friends. If you feel like putting some distance between you—either because you need it, or you think your BF/GF will need time to get over you—then honor that.

Sometimes, it's difficult to fully let someone go because, deep down, you don't want him/her to move on or stop loving you. But you've got to take the high road and let your ex go. It's not respectful to lead someone on or keep him/her in your life just because you feel guilty or want someone to fall back on.

Getting "Dumped"

If your BF/GF breaks up with you, it can hurt—bad. You might feel rejected, lonely, sad, and betrayed. But in the end, your self-respect is what really makes or breaks you. In other words, if you can walk away with your head held high instead of letting a breakup crush you, then you're keeping your self-respect intact.

When BFs/GFs don't want to be with you, they are, in a sense, helping you by letting you go. You deserve to be with someone who is totally into you. Maybe your BF/GF just figured out faster than you did that the relationship wasn't working. And hey, just because you're dumped, it doesn't mean you're trash. Your ex needed to move on for his/her own reasons, even if you think those reasons aren't good enough. If the breakup was delivered in a way that was totally disrespectful—like he/she sent a friend to tell you, just stopped calling, or suddenly had a new love interest—that still isn't a measure of your worth. (But your ex did blow it by not being honest or giving you the basic consideration you deserve!)

If your ex is honest about why he/she is breaking up with you, listen closely to any feedback offered. Or, after the sting is gone, if you think your ex will be kind and thoughtful about it, you might ask, "What *really* happened?" In other words, is it possible to turn the breakup into a lesson about how to make your next relationship better?

Although your heart may be aching, remember that you *do* matter. Know that you have a unique place on earth and a mission (whatever it may be) to fulfill. There are still tons of people out there who will appreciate who you are on the inside and love you for it!

After the Breakup

The breakup may be final, but the respect should go on—meaning you need to respect your ex's right to have a life apart from you, especially if he/she doesn't want to stay friends. Don't try to prevent your ex from seeing other people or spread nasty rumors about his/her new crush. You may be tempted to get back at him/her for the pain you're feeling, but this won't help you move forward. Instead, focus on yourself and your friendships—let the old relationship go.

If your ex disrespects you after the breakup or if the "Let's be friends" arrangement isn't working for you, you can set a boundary like:

"I respect your right to move on and date other people, and I expect you to give me the same consideration."

"I need you to give me more space. It will take time for me to get over this." (**Then set rules—in a respectful way—for when he/she can contact you.**)

"Being friends isn't working out for me. I still have feelings for you, so please don't call me or contact me anymore. I'll let you know when I'm feeling better and feel OK talking to you."

"I feel like our friendship means something more to you than it does to me. I don't want to lead you on or make you think that we'll get back together."

If the disrespect turns into full-blown harassment at school, check out Chapter 11 for tips on what to do. Or if you need help with other boundary violations and ways to get through the breakup, talk to an adult you trust.

Taking Care of You

Whether breaking up was your choice or not, you'll have a lot of emotions to sort through. You'll probably feel down for a while before you feel great again, especially if your self-respect was bruised by the breakup. If you're really upset for more than a few weeks, get some help by telling an adult what you're going through.

To focus on your personal passions, instead of passions of the heart, you can:

Think. Breakups help you learn about yourself and what you want in a relationship. Write feelings down. What did you learn? What will you do differently next time?

Chill. Spend time on your own (but not all the time), treat yourself with care, and do things you love to keep your mind-body connection strong. Take care of the basics, making sure to get the food, exercise, and sleep you need.

Hang out. If you're lonely, spend time with people you care about and have some fun. (Your BF/GF wasn't the only person to make you laugh, right?) If you ditched your friends and family to be with your BF/GF, you might have to do some apologizing to get those relationships back on track. These people care about you, and they'll forgive you for mistakes and, hopefully, support you when you need it most (now).

Talk to a pro. If you feel you're dwelling on the breakup a lot and need help dealing, consider talking to a school counselor or a professional therapist, if possible.

Relationship Savvy?

Use your journal to help you test your relationship IQ.

I want a BF/GF because: _____

I think I'm ready for a relationship because: _____

I'm looking for these traits in a BF/GF: _____

My relationship boundaries and deal-breakers are: _____

In my relationships, I make sure that my rights are honored by: _____

I've learned from my past relationships that: _____

Sex and the Respect Connection

One thing we learned as we were facing sexual choices is that there's more to safe sex than the physical stuff: Sex without self-respect is never safe. Becoming sexually active requires the same basics you always need when making choices: You've got to know yourself, trust yourself, and communicate confidently about what you want and need. If you don't have these essentials, you may struggle with how you feel about yourself after getting intimate. According to experts, girls are more likely than boys to link sex with depression and a loss of self-respect.[1]

If you're one of the 47 percent of teens who report that they're having sex,[2] then you already know that sexual activity brings up a lot of choices. There are straightforward choices, like how to protect yourself against sexually transmitted diseases (STDs) or unwanted pregnancy. And there are emotional choices, too, including when and if you're ready for sex (not just the first time but every time) and what your boundaries are. You'll also need to think about practical issues, like how you'll make decisions with a clear head (unlike the 25 percent of sexually active teens who say they drank alcohol or used drugs before their last sexual encounter).[3]

The bottom line? Many of your rights—from listening to your true feelings to staying safe—come up when you're making decisions about sex. Sexual activity can affect your self-respect and your relationships (not only with your partner but with family and friends, too). If sex is a part of your life, has been, or might be someday, then we hope you'll remember this essential part of your sex education: Sex is *always* a choice, and it's always connected to respect.

—Courtney & Andrea (the authors)

8

Sex

Girls have a lot on their minds when it comes to s-e-x. Even if you're not getting intimate, sex and sexuality are probably a part of your world in *some* way. After all, many girls are tuned in to how their bodies are changing, bringing up new feelings and sensations, thanks to all those puberty-induced hormones (which start as early as age 8 for some). Surrounded by sex-driven movies, TV shows, and music videos, girls often get the idea that being in a relationship means you *have* to have sex—or that sexual activity should become a part of your life in the teen years because it's a part of growing up. This is *so* not true.

What *is* true is that your sexual choices—who, what, when, where, why, and how—are *yours* to make. (Of course, your family probably influences your thinking about it, too.) And here's the deal: These choices, like all of your choices on the path to independence, are tied to how much you respect yourself. Intimacy and sex aren't just about biology, chemistry, and turn-ons. Sexual intimacy is a form of communication. And  sex, as you might have guessed or learned yourself, is an intense way of expressing yourself. That's because you're letting someone into your most personal and sacred space: your body, which includes your heart.

Many girls say they want to be physical with a partner (boyfriend/girlfriend/friend/crush) because they want to be closer to the person. These girls say they think about having sex because they want a heart-and-body bond with someone they either care about, like, or love. And they hope to get that same feeling back from their sexual partner. Maybe you've felt this way yourself. Wanting to be close to somebody is natural (many of us want this). But physical intimacy tends to make you vulnerable. Your feelings could get hurt more easily, especially if you're not in touch with how you feel about sex, what your body is ready for, and how you want to be treated by your partner.

Your "first time" or early sexual experiences have a huge effect on your self-respect. Many girls and young women say, frankly, that their first sexual experiences were something they'd rather forget. Either they didn't want it, felt they were too young emotionally, weren't sure, didn't feel comfortable, were impaired by drugs or alcohol, or were rejected or hurt by their partner afterward. You don't have to be an expert to figure out that experiences like these can lead to regret and self-doubt. But you might be surprised to learn that negative emotions can stick around for a long time afterward, leaving girls with feelings of low self-worth and messed-up ideas about sex. Sex isn't a bad thing, but sex without respect can leave you confused or hurt.

For many girls, sex comes down to a question of "Will I or won't I?" Nothing is ever this black or white. Waiting for the right time, age, or person is a big part of the equation, but you also have to ask yourself when you're *emotionally* ready to have sex—and that's more complicated. This is something to consider not just the first time but *every* time you become sexually active with someone, even if it's the same person for the rest of your life. Your mind and body can't be separated, so getting involved sexually isn't only a physical decision. Ideally, you need to make your choices based on whether you're ready—body, mind, and heart—to handle everything that comes with sexual activity.

It helps to think of being ready as getting to know yourself inside and out. Research shows that for young women to have a strong mind-body connection, they need to learn about sexuality in terms of their own pleasure, and not just in terms of risk factors and relationships.[4] Yet, girls are often taught about sexuality only in the context of reproduction (that you can get pregnant), risks (that you can get an STD), and heterosexual relationships (that you should be in love with, married to, or sexually attractive to the opposite sex).[5]

In other words, you aren't, for the most part, encouraged to acknowledge your own sexual desire when it surfaces. Starting at a young age, you're given messages from society and media that you should please and hold on to a guy by being sexually attractive or active. Many young women learn that they're supposed to accommodate someone else's sexual desire before they figure out their own needs, boundaries, or sexual identity (such as being lesbian or bisexual). Talk about mixed messages! And what does this mean for you? Not being in touch with your sexual feelings can make it harder for you, at any point in your life, to engage in sexual relationships that are healthy, consensual (both partners want it), pleasurable, and respectful.

> I didn't know what to do, even though I didn't like it. I didn't know how to say "Stop."
> —Noelle, 15

The fact remains: Not knowing yourself and what you want is risky business. You have to put your self-respect first by being honest with yourself about your sexual feelings and boundaries. When it comes to getting physical, your mind-body connection needs to stay strong—you can't let your body do all the talking. Of course, that's not as easy as it sounds. When you're in the heat of the moment, the chemicals released in your body can sway you to act now and think later. Even if it's difficult, you and your partner need to be open with each other at every step, or "base," along the way.

There will always be times when experiences in life don't live up to your expectations, or they leave a bigger imprint on you than you thought they would. Still, you can figure out what's right for you when it comes to sex—even if it's years off in the future—by always remembering your rights and "The 7 Respect Basics" (page 6). That means making choices based on listening to your gut, defining your boundaries, speaking up, and expecting to be treated as an equal in your relationships. With your self-respect firmly in place, sex will still be a big deal. But it will be a big deal that you'll be better equipped to handle emotionally and physically, now and for the rest of your life.

It's a CHOICE You Make

Most girls and women find that they feel most comfortable with getting physical or having sex when they know, trust, and respect themselves and their partners. Studies show that sexual experiences can have a negative effect on girls if these basics are missing. For example, without trust, it's hard to ask for what you want, to feel comfortable with what you're doing, or to have the courage to ask about your partner's sexual history so you can stay safe.

reTroSPECT: SHHH, IT'S NOT OK TO TALK ABOUT FEMALE SEXUALITY

It has long been considered taboo for girls and women to feel sexual desire, let alone talk about it. Sex has historically been a male domain, where guys are free to want sex, go after it, and talk about it (even in the most disrespectful ways). Females, on the other hand, have historically been told to stay pure and to stay quiet. To express sexual desire or act on it outside of what is socially acceptable can still get a girl labeled as a "slut" or "ho."

Today, many females do have more sexual liberation, but talking frankly about female sexuality still causes quite a stir. For instance, when Eve Ensler's widely acclaimed play *The Vagina Monologues* hit the scene in the late '90s, she made audiences shift in their chairs by talking openly about the private (and true) sexual thoughts and observations of women young and old. Ensler even asks her audiences to participate in the play by speaking and shouting about (gasp!) vaginas. The play isn't only about breaking taboos, though—every year, it's performed to raise money to end violence against women. And before Ensler, there was Judy Blume. Her 1970 children's book *Are You There God? It's Me, Margaret* has become not just a classic but a common rite of passage for girls. But when it was first released, the book was hotly debated because sixth-grader Margaret thought about things like her period and whether she would ever fill out her training bra.

These controversial works prove that the simple act of talking about female sexuality can always make some people uncomfortable. But if females aren't free to discuss their sexuality, it's a barrier to getting the respect they deserve—because to get respect, you have to be able to speak up. And teens totally agree they need more speaking up about sex. In a national survey, an overwhelming 88 percent of teens said that it would be easier for them to avoid pregnancy or to postpone sexual activity if they were able to have more open, honest conversations about these topics with their parents.[6]

Just like Eve Ensler, Judy Blume, and other trailblazers, you can strive to get more respect by taking the most daring step of all when it comes to your sexuality: talking about it.

Whether you need to be in love, in a committed relationship, married, or none of the above before you get physical or have sex is up to you. But mutual trust and respect can be the difference between you and your partner being ready for sex and other forms of intimacy, or being filled with regret afterward. When you're making a decision about getting physical, be sure to think *each and every time* about your options, boundaries, feelings, safety, and self-respect.

Your family, spiritual values, or sexual education program at school may influence your choice about when you're ready (or not ready) for sex. Studies show that 94 percent of adults believe that teens should be given a strong message from society not to have sex until they're at least out of high school.[7] Without a doubt, adults have their reasons for trying to protect and guide you. They have experience, after all, and have probably seen how taking sex lightly can lead to painful outcomes. Still, to understand what sex means to you and what you're ready for, you have to explore *your* personal beliefs about sex. Ultimately, it's a personal choice because your body and heart belong to you and no one else. There's not a one-size-fits-all formula for everyone. To make decisions with a clear head, keep asking yourself questions about what *you* want, need, and feel ready for.

What Are Your Beliefs and Values?

How you feel about sex (like a lot of issues in your life) starts with your values. Sex is a highly charged issue in society, especially when it comes to teen girls and young women. Your dad or mom might have told you not to have sex until marriage but, on the other hand, your boyfriend/girlfriend (BF/GF) might be pressuring you to ignore that advice.

So, the question is, what do *you* believe is right for you? This is your self-respect and your body on the line, after all. Ask yourself:

- What outside values and beliefs (such as those set by your family or religion) do you think should affect your decision to be sexually active or not?

- In your culture or community, what does it mean to be a girl who's sexually active? Do you agree with this point of view?

- Do you want to be a certain age, or at a certain point in your life, before you become sexually active? Why?

- Do you want to be in love or best friends with your sexual partner? Why is (or why isn't) this important to you?

- Are you comfortable with your sexual identity (whether you're straight, lesbian, or bisexual)? Or are you unsure about it? Do you need to explore your feelings further or get some advice?

Examining your beliefs—what sex means to you and how you want it to be a part of your life or not—will help you decide something really important: your sexual boundaries. And that's the next big question to ask yourself.

 If you're questioning your sexual identity and don't feel comfortable talking about it with people you know, don't go it alone. It might all seem confusing or like the world is against you, but there are people who care and can help. See pages 214–215 for a list of helplines, Web sites, organizations, and books for gay, lesbian, bisexual, transgender, or questioning (GLBTQ) teens.

What Are Your Boundaries?

You need to know your boundaries not only when deciding about sexual intercourse but also when considering *any* level of intimacy (kissing, touching, oral sex). Before you try something new, which can make anyone feel more vulnerable, be sure that you know yourself really well, trust your partner fully, and both understand what a respectful relationship is all about. If you want to take good care of your mind and body, then casual sex and advanced experimenting aren't safe introductions to getting physical. (You wouldn't be able to handle a turbo racecar just because you got your driver's license!) Basically, you need a foundation before you can safely try or test the limits of any activity.

Girls who skip all the bases and slide right into sex have an increased risk of STDs, pregnancy, and depression. Why depression? For starters, it can feel like a major shock to your system to give yourself in such an emotional and physical way. Afterward, you might feel degraded or dishonored in some way because, in your heart, you wanted more respect than casual sex could give you. Or you might have regrets about putting your body in harm's way if you don't know your partner's sexual history.

If sex is something you want to try in order to be liked, to fit in, or to be popular, those reasons shouldn't pass your gut checks. So, go at a pace that's right for you, consider the consequences of going too fast, and never ignore your doubts. It all comes down to knowing your boundaries and staying true to them.

What Do You Know About Your Body?

To make thoughtful choices about your sex life, you need to know how your body functions and what's happening when you get physical. You might be thinking, "Oh, I already know all about this stuff." But do you really? What's taught from school to school, from family to family, or from friend to friend can vary a lot. The information you've been given may not be as complete or accurate as you thought.

Maybe you've taken a sex education class that included everything from how your sexual response system works (like what can cause those tingling sensations when you get physical) to why sex sometimes hurts physically. Or maybe a parent has explained the basics of menstruation (your period) and how you become pregnant. Some schools and families suggest abstinence (avoiding sexual intercourse) until marriage, but those lessons don't explain everything about your actual *anatomy*. And if you're learning about your body from TV, movies, magazines, or books, the information can be helpful or harmful, depending on the source.

It's important to find out *everything* you can about your body. Ever hear of the uterus, ovaries, or vulva? In case you don't know, these aren't planets in the solar system but essential parts of the female anatomy. You need to learn all about your genitalia (the stuff on the outside) and your reproductive organs (the stuff on the inside) if you're going to be sexually active—or even if you're not. To really know your body, you can read about the female sexual response cycle, which explains what physically happens before, during, and after getting intimate or having sex. Check out some of the resources on pages 214–215 and talk to an adult if you still have questions. Always look to more than one source when you need info about your health and safety, so you're sure to get a more balanced set of facts.

Knowing yourself inside and out will lessen the chance of having sexual encounters that "just happened" but didn't feel right later on. Your body is yours for keeps: Get to know it intimately before you consider getting intimate with someone else.

SISTERHOOD

If you explore your sexuality in a self-respecting way, you're being a strong role model for other girls. Their decisions might be different from yours, but what matters is that they see how much thought and care you put into your choices. Sexual activity is a personal decision as it relates to each girl's individual body, boundaries, and values. Never pressure other girls into your way of thinking (like making your friends feel like they'll be more mature by having sex or judging them if they're sexually active and you're not). Sisterhood is about listening to, understanding, and supporting other girls in making the best choices they can.

Do You Know the Risks?

There's no way around it: Sex comes with emotional and physical risks. To respect yourself, consider these risks (and your options) and take them seriously. Know the facts, know your needs, and make decisions that address both. Consider these questions so you can make well-informed, healthy decisions:

❧ Do you understand the facts and myths about getting pregnant? For example, you *can* get pregnant your first time, while you have your period, or if your partner "pulls out."

FYI: It Doesn't Hurt to Ask

You might already have a sexual health expert who's available to you around the clock and who really cares about your well-being: a parent. Yes, talking about sex with a parent can seem as scary or embarrassing as one of those dreams where you forgot to wear your clothes to school. But for many of you, your parents *can* be trusted, want to help, and are a great resource. If you think that a parent (or a trusted adult like an older sister or aunt) will be open to it, ask some questions about sex, including:

❧ What should I know about the health risks of having sex? What about the emotional risks?

❧ What do you know about sex now that you wish an adult had told you when you were my age?

❧ What makes a sexual relationship healthy and respectful?

❧ What are your concerns if I get into a sexual relationship, now or in the future?

❧ If I decide to become sexually active, how might that affect my relationship with you?

❧ Are there some boundaries/values that you think I should consider?

❧ Do you know about all the methods of birth control? Do you know how to get access to these methods? Will your partner play an equal role in protecting you against pregnancy?

❧ Do you know about sexually transmitted diseases, ways to limit risks (like using condoms), and what happens to your body and future health if you get infected? There's a popular misconception among teens that oral or anal sex is a safe alternative to traditional intercourse (but you *can* still get STDs).

❧ Do you know how to take care of your body once you've had any form of sex? When you become sexually active, you need to get annual pelvic exams, including a Pap test, so a doctor can examine your genital area and reproductive organs to be sure you're in good health and haven't contracted any STDs or infections.

Can You Speak Up and Be Honest?

Although sex is a form of communication, if you rely on physical messages alone to communicate your needs, you could end up with a lot of misunderstandings. In a healthy sexual relationship, each partner needs to be comfortable when talking honestly about what he/she wants or doesn't want. For instance, a lot of women say that at times in their life they have faked sexual pleasure because they didn't want to let their partner down, were too embarrassed to mention how they really felt, or didn't know how to tell their partner what *would* make them feel good. If sex is communication, then faking pleasure is dishonesty. You shouldn't have to lie about what feels good (or be afraid to speak up when something doesn't) just to make your partner feel better.

When you have open communication about getting physical, you can:

- talk to your partner about contraception, pregnancy, or what you're comfortable with physically

- ask questions about your partner's sexual history and what intimacy means to both of you

- set limits without being pressured for more than you're ready for

- feel free to say no or yes, or to change your mind about any aspect of sex

- tell or show your partner what you enjoy physically

- be honest about how you're feeling at any time

When you're able to speak freely, you'll build trust with your partner. And you'll probably feel more secure knowing that your sexual boundaries will be respected. If you're sexually active (or thinking about it), remember that it's also crucial to have a trusted relationship with a doctor, parent, guardian, or knowledgeable older girl (like a sister) so you can ask questions about your feelings and body, and get reliable advice.

> He used me for sex because he knew I liked him so much. I should have never hooked up with him, because we never really talked about how we felt. I want the next guy to respect me and never do anything to hurt me on purpose.
> —Melody, 15

Gut Check

We wish it weren't true, but sometimes people lie to get your trust. You can't control when people are purposely dishonest (like if they say they're committed to you when they really aren't, or they promise that they'll respect your privacy but then tell others about your most intimate moments). However, you *can* trust your gut. If someone smooth-talks you or makes a bunch of promises so you'll have sex, your gut will probably send you signals to stay on alert. So, check in with yourself and really listen. If you have *any* doubts about someone's intentions or truthfulness, don't silence those warning signs. Take the time to get to know the person better before you let down your guard.

Are You Being Pressured?

You probably wouldn't be surprised to hear that 89 percent of girls ages 15–17 report feeling "some" or "a lot of" pressure about sex.[8] Any time you're pressured to go against your boundaries or ignore your gut, that's a form of disrespect. If you've been honest about your feelings, then no one should hound you for sex or set deadlines for you. Don't promise to be ready by some date on a calendar, like the prom or a school holiday. That just creates more pressure and anxiety, possibly setting you up for a major letdown.

Here are some situations that don't ever add up to respect:

- ❖ You're pressured to have sex or forced into sexual acts.

- ❖ You're trying to make a BF/GF happy or to "keep" him/her, so you go against your gut checks.

- ❖ Your partner lies to you—like saying he/she loves you when it's not true—to convince you to have sex.

- ❖ You don't want to be left out, and because everyone else seems like they're having sex or talking about it, you decide to do it as a way to fit in.

- ❖ You did it before, and so you feel like you can't say no now (you *can*).

When you're getting physical, your mind-body connection gets super sensitive, letting you know "I feel comfortable," or "Whoa, I don't think I want to go there." So, if a partner asks you to go further than you have before, if you're considering hooking up with someone you just met, or if you're thinking of trying something sexual that you haven't ever done, *always listen to what your gut is telling you.* When a decision truly feels right to you, your stomach won't be tied in painful knots and

> My boyfriend said, "I want to be with you," and then asked me to have sex. And I said no. A week later, he sent his sister over to my house to dump me. I'm glad I didn't have sex with him.
> —Felicia, 14

your mind won't race a mile a minute with doubts. Instead, you should feel at ease and comfortable. But be sure you're clear and sober when making these decisions. Being under the influence of drugs or alcohol will affect your ability to do what's right for you.

Just so you know, having sex with someone to start a relationship or try to stay together never works in the long run. If you're in a relationship and your partner wants more than you're ready to give (or the other way around), this means the two of you aren't in sync. Sex isn't going to suddenly fix things between you or make you both feel the same way. Although thinking about ending the relationship might seem like the worst thing in the world, it could turn out to be the best thing. You may lose your partner, but you'll keep your self-respect—and you won't be pressured to do something you're not ready for and, as a result, probably wouldn't enjoy.

If you *are* being pressured and you're not sure what to say to your partner, check out the following scenarios for help:

"I can't wait any longer. Come on, let's do it."

Try: "I'm not ready, and I don't want to. When—and if—I feel ready, I'll let you know, and we can talk about it then."

"If you loved me, you'd have sex with me. This is how we can show our love for each other."

Try: "Just because I love you doesn't mean I have to have sex with you. To me, love doesn't equal sex, and you can have one without the other. And besides, if you loved me, you wouldn't want me to do *anything* that I'm not ready for."

"I know you've done it already—what's the big deal?"

Try: "So what if I've had sex before? Sex is a choice, not an obligation. I say when I'm ready—not you—because I respect myself."

"If you don't do it, I'm going to break up with you."

Try: "I won't be pressured or threatened into doing something I don't want to do. If you can't respect my boundaries, then you're right—we should break up."

"If you don't want it, why are you dressed like that?"

Try: "I like to dress this way sometimes because it makes me feel good. But my clothes aren't a signal for what I want sexually. No means no."

"I don't get why you're saying no—we've done it before."

Try: "Sex is a choice—every time—and I don't feel like it." Or "I have to be honest: I wasn't ready when we had sex in the past. Now I want to wait until I feel more comfortable with myself and with what sex means to me."

If you want, you can practice these scenarios with a friend first. That way, you'll feel stronger and more confident when you talk to your partner.

Are You Emotionally Ready?

Sex is a better experience if you're emotionally mature, but it doesn't *make* you more mature. This is a big misconception—that doing what adults do can make you grow up faster. It's true that some girls are mature for their age, and maybe that describes you. But even so, your *partner* may not be. For example, if you believe that a sexual relationship requires trust and respect, that's a sign of maturity. If your partner thinks that sex is only about physical pleasure and not about meeting your needs (emotional or otherwise), then the two of you aren't in agreement about what sex means. Only you can know what you're really ready for, but remember that sex isn't an all-access-pass to adulthood.

You'll know you're closer to being ready when you understand the risks and feel completely capable of taking responsibility for your choices. Other signs that you might be ready: You truly value yourself, and you're in a healthy, trusting relationship with someone you respect (and he/she respects you in return). Even if your self-respect and your relationship are strong, you still have the right to say no about getting sexually intimate. It's *always* your choice.

Some Do. Some Don't. Some Might.

Deciding what's right for you could take some time. There's no hurry. Your thoughts and feelings about sex will change as you grow. Even if you're already sexually active, take some time to reflect on what you've learned or what you want going forward. Start by answering some questions in your journal.

- My personal, religious, or cultural values when it comes to sex are:

- I can (or can't) be honest about my sexual activity because:

- I want to wait to get physical or have sex with someone because:

- If I'm going to have sex, I want to be in a relationship in which I feel:

- I feel comfortable talking about the following topics with a partner:

- I've learned the following about pregnancy, STDs, and my sexual feelings:

If you're considering having sex with your partner:

- What feels right about going further?

- _____ makes me feel scared or uncomfortable because:

- Do we trust and respect each other enough to get more intimate? Do I feel safe? Why or why not?

- Will going further go against my values and boundaries?

- What responsibilities come with going further? Are we ready for them?

- Do I feel any doubts? What are they?

If you're already sexually active:

- Sex makes me feel (physically and emotionally):

- Before, during, and after I get physical, I want to feel:

- I speak up about my boundaries in the following ways:

- I check in with myself each time I'm making a sexual choice by:

If you're considering something experimental:

- ❧ Trying _____ will (or won't) go against my boundaries because:

- ❧ My level of sexual experience is:

- ❧ My experiences so far have made me feel:

- ❧ By experimenting more, I expect to feel:

- ❧ The potential risks to my body and my feelings about myself could be:

Pillow TALK

Sometimes, it can seem easier to just "get busy" than to talk about sex and your boundaries with a partner. But if you're going to get physical, you've got to talk first. Remember: Sex can make you feel more vulnerable and sensitive, but whether you and your partner will become closer to each other isn't guaranteed. It depends on how trusting, honest, and respectful your relationship was before you got physical. It also depends on how you both feel after the fact, which you should talk about throughout your sexual relationship.

When you're communicating about sexual activity, always be:

Honest. First, be truthful with *yourself*. What do you really need in order to feel safe and loved? Why do you want to have sex? Will it give you what you really need? Make your feelings clear to your partner and be truthful about your expectations.

Firm. Don't apologize for what you want or make it seem like it's only a suggestion. When you have a physical or emotional need, talk about it and make sure your partner knows why it's important to you.

Sincere. Don't giggle, smile, or avoid eye contact when communicating your feelings or asking for what you need. Start with "I feel _____" or "I need _____" statements to get your point across.

To make sure your self-respect isn't put at risk by getting physical, talk about these issues with your partner:

Your feelings. Talk about how you both feel about getting intimate and whether it means the same thing to both of you. Why do you each want to get sexual or not? How do you both think sex will change your relationship? How will the two of you feel if you break up after being physically intimate? Be specific about how you both view your relationship and level of commitment—and how you want it to be *after* getting physical.

Your definitions. Just what *kind* of sex are you talking about? Be sure that you and your partner are both clear on your definitions, so there's no confusion.

Your responsibilities. Both you and your partner share equal responsibility in preventing pregnancy or protecting yourselves from STDs. How will you protect yourselves against possible infection? (If either one of you already has an STD, you need to talk about that so you can both make informed choices about getting physical.) What are your birth control options? What will you do if you get pregnant? And what are your beliefs about adoption or abortion? What might happen if the adults in your lives find out that you're in a sexual relationship?

Your needs. How will you show each other respect before, during, and after sexual activity? What do you need from each other to feel safe and secure in a physically intimate relationship? Can you both handle this responsibility?

Your rights. Every moment of physical intimacy and every sexual encounter is a choice for both people. You can change your mind in the heat of the moment, and you can stop once you've started—you don't *have* to go through with anything! That's your right, period. Even if you've had sex with someone once, twice, or many times, that doesn't mean he/she is entitled to it. If you feel like putting the sexual part of a relationship on hold for a while or you want to wait instead of getting intimate, tell your partner your feelings. If he/she still wants sex to be a part of the relationship and you don't, then you'll have to accept that it's probably time to move on. It hurts to break up, but it hurts more to go against your boundaries. You have to be true to yourself first: You are *your* partner for life.

When It DOESN'T Feel Right

Sometimes, girls have sex and then afterward feel a whole mix of negative emotions. If you find yourself in this situation, think about what happened and why the experience wasn't fulfilling. Your feelings are a sign of your doubts and that you're learning more about yourself. They're also an opportunity to take another look at your boundaries.

According to numerous studies, teen girls who have frequent sexual encounters that lack trust and real intimacy are more likely to have low self-worth or to have been neglected or sexually abused as children. A 2003 study found that girls who had sex at age 14 or under were more likely to smoke, use drugs and alcohol, and break the law—1 out of 10 also said their first sexual experience was unwanted.[9] That's why it's so important to get in touch with your feelings before you have sex again.

Here are some of the negative feelings girls describe and what you can do if you've felt the same way:

Shame/regret. Are you being raised with family or religious values that strictly warn against having sex during the teen years? If you've been taught rules about sex that you now feel you've broken, then you might be ashamed about your decision, especially if you've been taught that sex is shameful to begin with.

Gut Check

There is another reason why you might feel ashamed: being a victim of past sexual abuse, which can range from being exposed to pornography, to being molested, to being raped. Victims don't always remember the abuse, but it can have a lasting effect on them if they've never had a chance to deal with it or heal. Check your gut to figure out if something deeper might be going on and see Chapter 9 for information about abuse and getting help.

I feel bad about giving myself to people I didn't care about. Now I care about myself more and want more.
—Cindy, 16

Respect Rx: No matter what you've been taught, sex doesn't have to feel shameful. If you've made the right decision for yourself and you feel respected by your partner, there's nothing to be ashamed of. But if you agree with your family's values and feel like you've crossed a boundary and now regret it, that's another issue. Don't be hard on yourself—instead, look at what happened and why, and remember to speak up if the situation arises again. In the meantime, talk to people you trust and ask for their support as you work through your feelings.

Guilt. Female sexuality has long been both a hush-hush and provocative topic. For example, some people have been brought up to think that girls should stay "pure" or be virgins until they marry. Girls who lose their virginity before marriage may feel guilty about it and may also be labeled as "sluts" or "hos" as a result of their decision to become sexually active. Some girls even label *themselves* "sluts" if they've had sex or if they want to but feel like they shouldn't.

Respect Rx: If you've had sex and you feel guilty about it, find an adult or a close friend to talk to first. For now, put sexual activity on hold until you feel more secure. Beating yourself up over past mistakes never helps. Instead, look at what you'd like to change, forgive yourself, and move on with new boundaries in place. If you don't have a problem with your sexuality but other people have called you names, set boundaries and stay strong: You know who you really are inside, and that's what counts. (See Chapter 11 for more on dealing with slut rumors at school.)

Disappointment/emptiness. Were you dumped right after you finally had sex with your BF/GF? Did you feel like strangers afterward, instead of feeling closer? Maybe you were hoping to get more out of the experience than your partner could offer, or you were lonely and looking for comfort. Sex won't give you something that's missing from your life already, and if you're in search of acceptance or validation, a sexual encounter can't provide it. That's why it's natural to feel let down or disappointed when a sexual experience doesn't live up to your expectations.

Respect Rx: Think about how to get love in healthy ways that fill you up and keep you safe (instead of making you more vulnerable). Can you ask your family for what you need, turn to friends, or seek out a mentor? If you feel empty or rejected, definitely limit getting physical with your partner for a while. Instead, take it slow, one date or phone call at a time. Spend more time doing activities you love and hanging out with your closest friends. You'll feel stronger and more secure—and that's a great way to get past the disappointment and move on with your life.

Stay in Check

Sex is definitely a complicated topic. Trying to keep in mind everything that you need to consider can seem overwhelming. That's where a checklist comes in handy. Before you become sexually active or continue having sex, run through this list to help yourself make decisions that are respectful of your mind and body. If you can't check off each item on the list, you're probably not ready to be sexually active and you may need to take another look at your boundaries.

My Values

☐ Deep down, I feel comfortable with and confident about my decision to have (or not have) sex.

☐ I know what sex means to me and what has shaped my decision.

☐ My decision is in line with my values.

☐ I've thought about my sexuality, and I'm comfortable with myself.

My Boundaries

☐ I know what I will and will not do.

☐ I know how to be honest with my partner.

☐ I know what I will do or say if someone tries to cross my boundaries.

☐ I know how to ask for what I need in a straightforward, clear way.

☐ I know the physical and emotional risks of sex.

My Sex Education

☐ I'm familiar with my body and have learned about my sexuality.

☐ I have referred to several reliable resources for my sex education.

☐ I know about pregnancy, contraception, and STDs, and I've talked to my partner about these issues.

☐ I know how to enjoy my body in other ways besides being in a sexual relationship.

☐ I know trusted adults I can go to for more information and advice.

My Self-Respect

☐ I make decisions that are respectful of my body, mind, and heart.

☐ I listen to my gut, even when I'm experiencing strong emotions.

☐ I am honest with myself, and I trust myself.

☐ I know how to learn from mistakes (and not punish myself over them).

☐ My decisions about sex aren't based on pressure from my partner, friends, or media.

Part Three:

Taking Action

My Story of Abuse and Survival

There is something about me that few people know but that I want other girls to know if it will help them or save their lives. When I was 5 years old, a family member sexually abused me. The details of the abuse aren't what matter now. What matters is how it changed my life and how I felt about and treated myself after it happened.

Immediately after the abuse, I often felt like I wasn't inside my body—it was more like I was floating outside of it, like a watchful ghost. By the time I was 13, I felt completely out of touch with myself. I never thought about the abuse, which had stopped by then. Deep down, I felt like I was a bad person. I started to have sex with lots of guys, but they didn't really care about me. I didn't understand why I was doing this.

When I was a senior in high school, something happened that changed my life again. I was at a party and had almost passed out in one of the bedrooms when a good friend—someone I trusted—forced me to have sex, even though I said no. Afterward, he acted like I had done it voluntarily. I couldn't stop sobbing all night. The next day, I told a friend and she said there was a word for what he'd done: "rape." She helped me get help. I know now that it saved me.

It's taken a lot of counseling, but I'm starting to move on with my life, and I have stopped blaming myself. A lot was taken from me during those years, but I have now taken back the most important part: my self-respect. My hope is that all girls who have been abused can do the same. And that starts with getting help.

—T.J., 25

9

Dealing with Abuse

There is a kind of disrespect that is so hurtful and painful that most people don't want to talk about it. Often, it's a big, dark secret. The problem is abuse, and it's a violation of your right to be safe, to be treated as an equal, and to believe in your worth. The bottom line is that every act of abuse is a violation of every girl's birthright: respect.

Abuse may be physical, sexual, and/or emotional. And an abuser may be someone you know, like a family member, friend, or boyfriend/girlfriend (BF/GF). Most abuse is domestic, meaning it happens among people who live together, are related, know each other intimately, or are dating. But an abuser could be a stranger or someone you just met.

Despite many efforts to end violence and abuse, girls and women still make up the highest percentage of victims: 1 in 3 females worldwide have been emotionally, physically, or sexually abused.[1] We're not trying to scare you, but we do want you to know that the rights of many girls and women are being violated on a daily basis. And we (meaning every girl and woman) have a right to talk about it, to fight it, and to heal.

Abuse is *always* a big deal. It doesn't make a girl "tougher." No one deserves it. And no girl should feel like she has to "just get over it" without help and support. If you believe you've been abused, please seek help, even if the abuse took place long ago or if you're not sure what happened. On pages 204–206, you'll find a list of helplines, Web sites, and recommended reading. If you know a friend or family member who has been or is being abused, you can share these resources with her.

FYI: The Global Abuse of Girls

Violence against women and girls is a global issue, according to organizations like Amnesty International, which helps expose these violations and works to improve human rights. Some of the abuses in other parts of the world and closer to home include:

- Females who have been jailed or imprisoned (including teen girls) are often raped or sexually assaulted by the guards, who are rarely punished.

- Girls around the world are trafficked (bought and sold) by abusers who sometimes keep them locked up as sex or domestic slaves. Some of these girls are put in sweatshops where the conditions are terrible and the pay is incredibly low (or workers aren't paid at all). Other girls are sold to international pornography rings where they are not only abused but also, in some cases, murdered.

- Women and girls are treated as property in some countries. Brides are supposed to pay a large dowry (money promised to the groom's family) when they marry, and brides who can't pay may be beaten or killed by members of their new family.

- In some societies, women who are suspected of having an affair or having sex before marriage (including being raped) can be publicly stoned or legally murdered by their husbands or their brothers.

- More than 135 million girls in parts of Africa, the Middle East, and other regions have had some or all of their external genitalia cut off and stitched together again as part of a cultural ritual. This painful practice has infected many girls with HIV/AIDS or made them sterile (unable to have a baby).[2]

Studies show that abuse puts girls at increased risk for depression, suicide, psychological disorders, eating disorders, unwanted pregnancies, drug or alcohol addiction, and sexually transmitted diseases (STDs). Girls who have been sexually or physically abused are more than twice as likely as other girls to engage in risky sexual behavior.[3] In the end, abuse can affect a girl's relationships, dreams, and happiness—throughout her entire life.

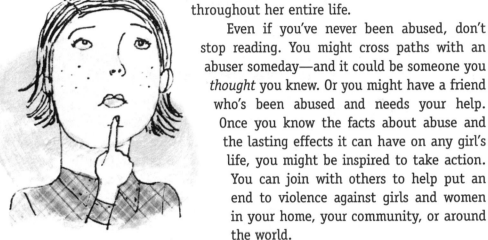

Even if you've never been abused, don't stop reading. You might cross paths with an abuser someday—and it could be someone you *thought* you knew. Or you might have a friend who's been abused and needs your help. Once you know the facts about abuse and the lasting effects it can have on any girl's life, you might be inspired to take action. You can join with others to help put an end to violence against girls and women in your home, your community, or around the world.

The FACTS

Every state or country has its own laws regarding abuse. However, based on federal laws in the United States and on definitions created by leading abuse-awareness organizations, here are the facts:

Emotional abuse is when someone uses words to hurt, shame, or control another person. Abusers insult or constantly put down their victims and call them names to make them feel worthless, fearful, or powerless. Other forms of emotional abuse include when parents or guardians threaten to harm their children or expose them to dangerous situations like illegal drug use and violent acts. In BF/GF relationships, emotional abuse may include stalking, extreme jealousy, threats of suicide or physical harm, and/or isolating the victim from family and friends. Studies show that one-third of teen dating relationships are abusive.[4]

Physical abuse is when someone's health or safety is put at risk. A family member or BF/GF can inflict the abuse, and it may include hitting, shoving, slapping, cutting, burning, kicking, choking, physically restraining the victim, or making threats with a weapon. If two people involved in an abusive relationship are romantic or intimate partners, it's called domestic or dating violence. According to one study, 40 percent of girls ages 14–17 say they know someone their age who has been hit or beaten by a boyfriend.[5]

Child molestation is when a child or teenager is forced or coerced (manipulated) by an entrusted adult or older youth to take part in pornography, prostitution, voyeurism (watching sexual acts), sexual talk, fondling, sexual kissing, touching of genitals or breasts, and/or vaginal, anal, or oral sex. It's estimated that up to half of girls who are molested are violated by a parent, a brother, or another person entrusted as a family member (such as a caregiver).[6]

Statutory rape is an illegal sexual relationship—even if it's consensual—between someone over age 18 and a minor (someone under age 18). This may include a sexual relationship with a teacher, a religious leader, a boss, a camp counselor, or older boyfriends/girlfriends. Research shows that 6 out of 10 girls who had sex before age 15 were coerced by males who were, on average, six years older.[7]

Sexual abuse, which includes some of the same acts as child molestation, is defined as rape, unwanted sexual contact, harassment, or touching by a stranger, a peer, or an acquaintance. Sexual assaults could include having your clothes ripped off, being exposed to the perpetrator's genitals (being "flashed"), or unwanted grabbing and fondling.

Rape is forced or nonconsensual sexual intercourse, including oral or anal sex, by a stranger, an acquaintance, a friend, or a family member (the majority of victims know their attackers, according to many studies). Rapists often use physical force, weapons, or intimidation, such as threatening to kill their victims. It sometimes involves the use of drugs that sedate the victim unknowingly (such as date-rape drugs slipped into a drink).

The Victim Isn't to Blame

When a girl is abused, the issue of blame often comes up: "Who is responsible?" And in so many cases—including court cases—people blame the victim. This should make girls everywhere really angry because it's unjust, unfair, and untrue. Blaming the victim creates an atmosphere of secrecy and shame. And fear of blame may make girls feel like they won't be helped or protected if they tell the truth about the abuse.

It's no wonder that many sex crimes go unreported. In fact, the most common reasons given for not reporting sex crimes are that the victims thought the abuse was a private or personal matter, or they feared revenge from the abuser. Some girls don't report an assault because they're afraid that they'll get in trouble for having broken some other rule at the time (such as staying out past curfew or drinking alcohol at a party). Because many incidents of abuse *aren't* reported, the number of victims is most likely even higher than estimated.

If you're ever emotionally, physically, or sexually abused, it's never your fault. Never. Abuse is about someone trying to get power and control. Many people who abuse others do so because *they* feel powerless or worthless (and perhaps they were made to feel that way by an abuser at some point in their childhood). Some abusers have other reasons behind their actions, including mental illness—but even so, *they* are still responsible for their actions. No matter what the motive or excuse may be, abuse is never the victim's fault and no one "asks for it." Abusers are always responsible for their actions and the pain they've caused.

Dating VIOLENCE

Emotional, physical, and sexual abuse happens in many romantic relationships. Dating violence can affect anyone regardless of age, sex, sexual identity, race, class, or mental or physical abilities. Maybe it has already affected you.

Some people wonder how a girl can be attracted to someone who's abusive or why she stays in the relationship. To a certain extent, that question goes back to the practice of blaming the victim. Girls are never to blame for being abused, but they may get caught in an abusive dating relationship for a number of reasons, including:

- being so beaten down emotionally or physically that they no longer realize the abuse is wrong, needs to stop, and *can* be stopped

- worrying that no one will protect them if they report what's happening

- fearing that the abuser will kill/punish them or come after their family members and friends

- believing, as a result of family abuse, that the relationship is normal or even the safer, more protective choice

❧ feeling like they somehow deserve the abuse or that it's proof of the abuser's love for them

❧ feeling confused about how people treat each other in a respectful relationship

No matter what the reason behind the victim's decision to stay, the *abuser* is the one who's breaking the law or violating a girl's rights. And that means the abuser is responsible for the abuse.

The Cycle of Violence

Sometimes, there are **red flags** (warning signs) that a person will become abusive or that emotional abuse will escalate into physical or sexual abuse. These abusive behaviors—even if they occur only once—are disrespectful and are reason enough to leave your BF/GF. Be on guard if he/she:

⚑ tries to control you or limit your independence, such as isolating you from friends and family

⚑ gets extremely jealous

⚑ stalks you and always seems to know your schedule and whereabouts

⚑ excuses his/her rages as "caring about you too much" or "being too in love with you"

⚑ verbally abuses you, such as calling you names or putting you down

⚑ has abused former girlfriends/boyfriends

⚑ disrespects or degrades other girls and women

⚑ tries to restrain you during an argument, like blocking your way or grabbing your arms so you can't leave

⚑ explodes with anger and makes threats that are aimed at you and other people, including your family

Every relationship is unique, but when a romantic relationship enters an abusive pattern, there's usually a predictable three-phase cycle that it follows, according to experts. Here's what it looks like:

#1 Tension-building phase: Your BF/GF tries to control you by making decisions for you or limiting who you can hang out with. He/she gets mad or jealous easily, or yells instead of talking calmly about minor disagreements. You try to keep the peace by pleasing him/her because you're afraid or don't want to fight.

#2 Explosion phase: Your BF/GF blows up at you during an argument and gets abusive in some way. Or he/she threatens or beats up someone else because of jealousy over you. During this phase, physical or sexual abuse is more likely to occur.

#3 Promises and presents phase: Your BF/GF tries to win you back or romance you with gifts, apologies, and promises never to hurt you again. During this phase, the abuse cycle sometimes starts all over again.

The cycle of dating violence usually keeps going until someone puts a stop to it. In some cases, dating violence escalates to the point where a girl or woman is severely injured—or even killed—by her abuser.

If you're in this kind of relationship, help is out there. Every day, girls and women do break the cycle of abuse by speaking out and getting support. Tell someone you trust (like a friend, parent, teacher, or school counselor) as soon as possible and seek information or resources to help protect yourself. The National Center for Victims of Crime (NCVC) offers advice on what to do if you've decided to break up with an abuser, including developing a safe exit plan (especially if you live with your BF/GF) and obtaining a restraining order that requires the abuser to stay away from you. You can reach the NCVC at 1-800-FYI-CALL (1-800-394-2255) or via its Web site at: www.ncvc.org. On pages 204–205, you'll find other helpline listings you can call for support.

IT HAPPENS . . .

I had a boyfriend who verbally abused me and tried to physically abuse me. He also didn't want me to talk to my best friend, who's a guy.—Myra, 14

My dad has set a bad example by abusing/hitting me to try to teach me right from wrong. All this has taught me is that violence is not the way to teach your children right from wrong.—Corina, 16

When my friend broke up with a guy, he told her that she was going to be with him no matter what, so he raped her right there, even though she said no.— Alesha, 16

My friend was in a verbally abusive relationship. Her boyfriend would always tell her what she could and could not do. And he often tried to make her believe what he wanted her to think. He didn't show her any respect at all.—Kimberlee, 15

I have a couple of friends who were date raped at parties where alcohol was consumed. They didn't do anything about it afterward, though.—Chantelle, 17

If you're ever in immediate danger, contact the police or seek help from a trusted adult. The sooner you can escape the pattern of dating violence, the sooner you can heal.

If You're Stalked

For many girls, part of the cycle of dating violence includes being stalked (however, a stalker could also be a stranger or an acquaintance). Stalking is a crime that's defined as a series of actions that make you feel afraid or in danger. For example, if someone:

- follows you

- damages your property

- ignores direct requests to stay away from you

- threatens you via the Internet, phone, or mail

- repeatedly drives by your home or calls you and hangs up

If you're being stalked, take it seriously. Don't wait until the situation gets worse or assume the stalker will lose interest. If you're in immediate danger, call the police. Otherwise, you can file a police report as soon as possible. You might be required to keep a log and evidence so the police will look into the case further. You also have the option of getting a court order that will help to keep the stalker away from you.

Be sure to tell your family and friends about every stalking incident. You can also alert your school's security staff and your boss if you have an after-school job. Create a safety plan by changing your routine and having places to go if you feel threatened at home, at school, or at your job. Keep working with the authorities to make sure that you're safe and the stalker is stopped.

I tried to treat my so-called "secret admirer's" frequent letters and phone calls like they were no big deal, all the while ignoring the nervous jump in my stomach. When I finally reported him, the police did act quickly and the guy was prosecuted. I rarely think or talk about him now, but when I do, I don't refer to him as my secret admirer. I call him what he was: a stalker.
—Margaret, 19

My Say

Why It Hurts

Thirteen-year-old Christine is a poet who loves to sing and act. But on the inside, she's in pain because her father verbally abuses her every day.

On verbal abuse:

"My father screams at me over little things, like leaving the light on. I don't get a fair say about how I feel—he'll insult me until he wins any argument. Once, I was sorting through a box of keepsakes until really late. I left my sorted piles in neat rows on the kitchen table and was planning to file them the next morning. But he got up before me and was mad about the mess. He yelled at my mother, which woke me up, and I was too afraid to go downstairs. I came down later and found all my stuff on the floor. He started yelling at me and calling me terrible names."

On how it feels:

"When he's hurting me, I tend not to say anything. I don't stand up for myself because I'm usually overpowered by all these feelings of hatred, and I'm afraid that something I say could be used against me."

On how she helps herself:

"Despite what my dad says, I still try to love myself. I talk to my best friend about my feelings, and she really listens to me. I also write poetry about how I feel. Mostly, I try to show respect to others, even when someone is in the wrong. My golden rule is to treat other people the way I want to be treated."

Family SECRETS

The facts show that abuse happens in families. This can be especially painful because families are supposed to love and protect you. If you've ever been hurt or watched one of your family members be abused, you know that it can leave you feeling scared, confused, ashamed, and unloved. Family abuse is a war—in your home and heart—that can cause you to lose confidence and faith in yourself.

reTroSPeCT: CHANGING LaWS, raISING awareNess

It wasn't until 1994 that the Violence Against Women Act was passed, making domestic violence a federal crime. Since that time, the law has been updated to help combat stalking, dating violence, and the trafficking of females for prostitution or slavery. To learn about how the law protects (or doesn't protect) you, check out the Office on Violence Against Women Web site (www.ojp.usdoj.gov/vawo) or get involved with V-Day (www.vday.org), a global movement to stop violence against girls and women. Go further by educating other girls in your community about the types of abuse, how to stop them, and how to get help. Check out page 194 for how a group of girls is taking action to do just that!

Studies show that the damage of abuse goes deep. Victims of family abuse are more likely to be victims in the future. Many girls who experience domestic violence in their homes suffer from low self-worth and depression. If you've witnessed women in your family being abused, you might believe this is the way females should be treated (but it's not).

You have a right to feel safe and loved, and you're worthy of being on this planet. Abuse is a violation of all of your rights. If someone in your family—a parent, guardian, sibling, cousin, grandparent, family friend, a parent's BF/GF, or an uncle or aunt—is abusing you or has in the past, talk to someone and get help. If you have family secrets like any of these, don't let them become your secret for life:

- You're put down, called names, or cussed out by family members.

- A family member manipulates you by lying, making threats, or exploiting you in some way.

- You're forced to live in dangerous conditions, you've been abandoned, or you don't have basic necessities like food, medical care, or shelter.

- Someone in your home abuses drugs or alcohol and, as a result, you're at risk or neglected.

- The adults at home are in a physically, emotionally, or sexually abusive relationship.

- A sibling beats you up or threatens you so often that you're scared almost all of the time.

- To discipline you, a family member or trusted adult uses physical punishment, which many experts say can be mentally and physically harmful.

- A family member has committed a crime against you—exposing you to inappropriate sexual activity or coercing/forcing you into sexual acts.

If any of these abuses are happening in your family, get help from an adult you trust. You can talk to a relative or close family friend—or confide in a teacher, school counselor, doctor, or religious leader.

Another option is to reach out to any of the national organizations on pages 205–206, where you'll find people who will listen and believe you. You can get detailed information on creating safety plans (such as what to do if a family member is being beaten), getting medical attention, and reporting abuse. If the abuse has stopped, you can still report it. You will likely need to seek the support of a therapist or counselor who can help you recover and regain any self-respect that you've lost.

SPEAK UP

It takes a lot of courage to tell someone you've been abused. Just getting those words out can be hard enough. But in some cases, girls find that the person they've confided in doesn't believe them. Maybe this has happened to you. Please don't let this stop you from finding another source of help. Call a helpline: The people who answer the phones are trained to help someone who's in a difficult situation like this. Don't give up!

Sexual ASSAULT

Rape is one of the most devastating things a girl could endure. Even though rape is a sexual assault, it is not about sex. Rapists want to get power, and they get it by making someone else (their victim) feel powerless. It doesn't matter what a girl was wearing or doing at the time of the rape—she's not responsible for it. And it doesn't matter if the abuser used a condom or knew the victim—it's still an assault because no one has the right to force a girl into sexual acts against her wishes or without her knowledge. The truth remains: The victim is never to blame.

Often, victims think that no one will believe them or that they'll be blamed for what happened (making them less likely to report the incident). It can be particularly confusing if the abuser is a friend or BF/GF. In the case of a rape, there are many organizations that can help you, no matter how complicated your situation might be (see the list on pages 204–206).

If you're ever in a rape situation, always try to put your safety first. That might mean defending yourself or fleeing your attacker. Once you've reached a safe place, you can take the following actions, even if you just *think* something happened but you can't completely remember:

❧ If you want to report the abuse or rape, don't take a shower, change clothes, or clean up in any way after the incident. (This helps preserve any evidence of the assault.) Although your first impulse might be to wash away what happened, you might end up washing away the evidence. Contact the police if you want to report the crime.

SISTERHOOD

If you know a girl who's being abused, you can help her in a few ways. (1) Get her to a safe place. (2) Listen to her without passing judgment or placing blame. Let her know you believe her and want to help. (3) Empower her to find help, including getting medical attention and counseling. Together, contact a trusted adult or a crisis helpline. Offer to make the call for her, if she wants you to. (4) If she's reluctant to get help, talk to an adult confidentially and ask for support.

❧ Tell a trusted friend or an adult who can go with you to get immediate medical attention, preferably in a hospital emergency room. Ask for a rape kit exam, which gathers evidence in case you want to prosecute the abuser (be sure to ask the doctor about your confidentiality rights first). If you believe you were drugged or sedated before the assault, ask to be tested for substances in your body within 24 hours of ingestion.

❧ If you're afraid to talk to someone you know, call a crisis helpline. You can find the numbers of these helplines in a phone book or use the list on pages 204–205. A crisis counselor can guide you through your options, such as how to get immediate medical attention.

❧ After the assault, no matter what other actions you've taken, talk about your feelings to someone—a doctor, therapist, counselor, or trusted adult.

Trauma and HEALING

Most people who experience abuse also experience trauma (a form of shock that can have long-lasting emotional effects). Often, victims of abuse bury or block out traumatic events to protect themselves and to survive. But the trauma is still recorded deep in the brain, as if it were under lock and key.

In fact, a deeply buried trauma can influence your thoughts and behaviors for a long time after it occurred. Intense emotions may be triggered in your daily life by a word, a situation, a scent, or a sound. You might be unexpectedly reminded (in the form of a flashback or feeling) of something that hurt you and hasn't yet healed.

If you're a survivor of abuse or you're feeling threatened by violence around you, remember that there *are* people and organizations available to help you deal with the trauma and pain. We hope you'll reach out, because you're worth it.

Acknowledging Abuse

If you've experienced abuse, you know it can be difficult to admit the abuse to anyone, maybe even to yourself. Many survivors of abuse deny it, try to erase it from their memory, or insist that it made them a stronger person. But abuse always affects your self-respect, so find the courage to seek help so you don't get trapped in a pattern of abuse now or in the future.

If it feels safe for you to do so, write in your journal about the abuse:

❧ Describe the moment of abuse and how it made you feel. You might want to draw pictures of it instead, using images and symbols that describe your feelings.

❧ Write what you wished you could do about it at the time.

❧ Write what you can do now.

Recording your thoughts about the following can be healing:

❧ Do you believe you need to report any of the abuse? Do you want to report it?

❧ Do you want to talk to a counselor or therapist and explore the abuse further? Why or why not?

❧ Do you need to find help to protect yourself right now? Who can help?

Some people call this type of reflection "writing the wrongs." What you decide to do after you've explored your feelings is up to you. Remember: Getting help is a respect basic.

How a Self-Defense Class Changed My Life

As a young child, Medea (now 13) was abused, which did some major damage to her self-respect, confidence, and ability to set boundaries. But now she's more open to adventure and taking risks, thanks to a self-defense class created for teen girls, which taught her how to protect herself. Here, Medea talks about why she thinks all girls should learn to defend themselves.

On the secret to self-defense:

"Using your voice is such a big part of defending yourself—our voices are so powerful. Even if you can't totally fight back with your whole body, you can use your voice to try to stop an attacker."

On setting boundaries:

"I feel like I'm not as much of a pushover because of the self-defense class. I can now say no with confidence. There have been a couple times when strangers have touched me on my leg or said something to me, and I was able to say, 'Stop. Don't do that to me.'"

On walking strong and confident:

"I was a really insecure person until the class—I'd never walked in a way that showed I'm powerful and strong. Now when I feel like I'm in danger, the first thing I do is walk strong. This reaction just clicks in when I feel unsafe, and people see me differently—as someone not to mess with."

On the payoff:

"Taking a class helps you so much, emotionally and physically. You feel so much better about yourself. Even if you're already confident, you'll feel even better after learning self-defense. Being able to rely on yourself for protection is amazing. You feel like you are your own bodyguard."

10

Defending Yourself

There's something irresistibly empowering about all those movies, comic books, and TV shows starring a new kind of superhero: the girl who knows how to kick some bad-guy butt. What makes these strong females so appealing? Probably the fact that most of us don't have role models like that in real life. You *do* have the power to protect yourself, though—in many ways. You just need to learn how to show your power, so you can fight for your rights and defend yourself if push comes to shove.

You may have grown up learning that a girl isn't supposed get angry or be tough. If so, you might feel unprepared if you're ever in a dangerous situation. But you can be ready. When you wear your self-respect on your sleeve, that kind of confidence could help prevent you from becoming a victim. And when you arm yourself with self-defense techniques designed especially for young women, you'll learn the skills to help stop an attack. We're not only talking about attacks by strangers on the street—it's possible to be assaulted by someone you know (or just met) in a place where you normally feel safe.

SPEAK UP

If someone does get past your boundaries and overcomes you, it's *not* your fault. Don't blame yourself. Instead, fight back in another way: Tell someone you trust and get help.

You have a right to feel safe, and part of *feeling* safe is building your confidence and strength so you'll know what to do if you ever are in a risky situation and need to protect yourself. Even if you know your boundaries, listen to your gut, and let others see your strength, you could still benefit from learning self-defense skills. These techniques can help you to discover the power of your own voice and to take a stand, literally, that may stop attackers in their tracks. The "defense" in "self-defense" is about sticking up for and protecting yourself.

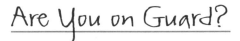

Are You on Guard?

If you were raised with the idea that girls shouldn't be strong, then you might not feel sure about learning to defend yourself. On the other hand, if you've been taught to be aggressive, you might feel uncomfortable with the nonviolent communication tools you're about to learn. Keep in mind where you're coming from as you find your strength and learn to use it in new ways. Explore these questions in your journal:

Have you been allowed to express anger? How so?

When you're threatened, how do you respond?

With people you know, do you lash out when you feel defensive instead of talking calmly?

Are you more aggressive or timid? Why do you think you're that way?

Are you afraid of what other people will think of you if you use some self-defense moves or verbal boundaries? Why or why not?

Find and Show Your POWER

You might think that you have to be physically strong to have real power or to fight back if someone tries to hurt you. But your actual power is the fight within you—your will to survive. And it starts not with your fists but with assertiveness (a.k.a. being bold and confident) and trusting your gut.

When a girl's senses are sharp and her confidence is on display, an attacker will often pass her by. That's because an assertive girl is more likely to defend herself, yell or run for help, or go to the police. If you ever need to defend yourself, having this kind of power is the real force that should always be with you.

Criminals on the lookout for victims say they usually seek girls and women who don't seem assertive. This is why assertiveness is a key ingredient in preventing an assault from happening. It's estimated that nearly half of all assaults are prevented or ended because of *assertiveness alone.* [1] But being assertive doesn't mean being aggressive or picking fights. Your goal is to avoid violence, not stir it up.

So, how can you build this skill? It's all about being aware of your body language, using your voice, and taking a stand to enforce your boundaries.

> I used to think people could be in my space and it wasn't a big deal, because people have been in my space my whole life. Now I know that I can tell people, "You're in my space, and I don't want you there."
> —Melinda, 13

Be Aware of Your Body Language

Did you know most communication has nothing to do with talking? Even before you open your mouth to speak, you send out messages with your body language (facial expressions, mannerisms, posture). When you feel confident, your body language shows it: You walk tall with purpose, and you aren't afraid to look around you.

Want to know if you look assertive? When you're out in public and see your reflection in a window, pay attention to your body language. Or have your mom, dad, or a friend (one who won't make you feel self-conscious) watch you from a distance and give you feedback. Does your body language reflect the descriptions below? Do you:

- look **comfortable, purposeful, and confident** or confused, uneasy, or intimidated?

- look like **you own the space around you** or use as little space as possible, like you're shrinking into a corner?

- **hold your head up and look around** or stare at the ground?

- have a **straight back and confident posture** or slouch?

- **swing your hands confidently by your side** or hold your arms and hands close to your body as if you're nervous?

- **walk with a firm stride** like you know where you're going, or appear hesitant?

Confident body language tells people, "I'm strong, and I believe in myself." And it shows that you're assertive.

Make Eye Contact

Wherever you go, always try to look people in the eye with confidence. At times when you feel threatened—like when you cross paths with someone who seems dangerous—your reaction might be to look away from the person in the hope that you won't be noticed. Or you might think that making eye contact with the person is like giving an "invitation" for him/her to talk to you. But that actually depends on what *type* of eye contact you make: Eyes can say everything from "I'm shy and nervous" to "Leave me alone!"

If you *do* feel threatened, maintain a calm, steady gaze that sends the message that you're paying attention and you don't get intimidated easily. Don't smile or look down—this could be interpreted as friendliness or submission. Keep making assertive eye contact to send the message that you're bold and strong. Then quickly walk toward a safe place to get away from the person.

Power Up Your Voice

An assertive voice is one of your best self-defense weapons because it helps you to command attention. If an attacker or someone you know tries to hurt you, you can use your voice to yell for help or to show that you're not going to back down. Here are some ways to practice showing your power:

Pay attention to your pitch: Watch the TV news to listen to how an anchorwoman speaks. Or study how Oprah Winfrey talks: She's the poster-woman for assertiveness! These women sound professional and confident, not squeaky or uncertain. You can mimic their tone while talking to the mirror or into a tape recorder.

Sound like you mean business: Sometimes, girls "ask" nicely instead of setting a clear boundary (for example, "Take your hand off my leg, OK?"). Don't end your sentences like you're asking a question because you'll sound unsure. *Assertive* boundaries end with a period. To practice setting boundaries, you can ask an adult to role-play with you and to point out when you sound like you're questioning instead of being firm.

Practice yelling "NO!" with power: Yelling with power isn't about screaming or raising the pitch of your voice like a desperate victim in a horror movie. Have you ever heard the way that military officers speak during drills (in real life or in the movies)? Your goal is to yell "NO!" with that kind of power but with a little less "bark." Think of it like singing opera or cheerleading: You need to yell from your diaphragm—your gut—not from the top of your throat, so you sound forceful and commanding.

For practice, yell "NO!" seriously, loudly, and with conviction. Do it as loud and strong as you can, until you scare yourself or someone in the other room with your assertiveness. (Just warn your family ahead of time that you're practicing and not being attacked for real.) To hear an example of how to say no with power, go to the *Respect* Web site at www.respectgirls.com.

Here are some situations many girls have been in that didn't pass their gut checks, along with examples of what and what not to do. If you find yourself in a situation like the ones described here, always opt for the assertive response. Avoid being passive (in other words, don't let people walk all over you) because you might seem like an easier target. On the other hand, don't come off as overly aggressive because you might provoke the person, and the situation could escalate.

A guy on the street says, "Smile," and when you don't he barks, "What's wrong with you? Don't you like me?"

Passive response: You smile or say, "No, it's not that, I'm sorry. I was just thinking about something."

Aggressive response: "Why should I, jerk?"

Assertive response: "I don't want to smile. Leave me alone."

You're home alone, and a salesperson rings your doorbell and says, "I just need a few minutes of your time to show you this product."

Passive response: "OK, as long as it doesn't take that long."

Aggressive response: "Show some other fool—you're wasting my time."

Assertive response: "I don't need any products. I'm not interested. Good-bye."

A person who asks you for spare change gets pushy when you say no. He/she presses you with, "Oh come on, don't you have some money for someone who's down and out?"

Passive response: "OK, I guess, let me see what I have."

Aggressive response: "Not for you—get a job!"

Assertive response: "I already told you that I can't help you."

A guy you met at a school game corners you in the parking lot later, saying, "Come on, I want you to go somewhere with me."

Passive response: You giggle and shake your head.

Aggressive response: "In your dreams."

Assertive response: "No—I'm going home now. My family is waiting for me."

Someone starts talking to you while you're reading a book at the bus stop. When you don't respond, she says: "Hey, I'm talking to you!"

Passive response: "Uh, were you talking to me? I didn't hear you, sorry."

Aggressive response: "So what? Get lost."

Assertive response: "I don't want to talk right now."

Stand Strong

In many situations, a force of nature seems to take over when you're attacked or threatened. Your body and mind want to instantly react by either running away or fighting to defend yourself. This reaction to perceived danger is known as the "fight or flight" response. Your instinct might be to stand up to your attacker or run away, both of which can help you stay safe.

If someone oversteps your boundaries or if you're surprise attacked, meaning you didn't see the person coming, remember your assertiveness and put it into action. Whether the person is a stranger or someone you know, trust your instincts. Take the following steps to defuse (turn down the intensity of) the situation or to defend yourself:

I feel so much safer and more confident in myself now that I know how to defend myself.
—Camille, 11

#1 Hold your ground. If you're standing up when you're threatened, don't teeter back and forth or back up, as this might make you look scared or easy to knock over. Plant your feet firmly on the ground about hip-width apart, and put your hands up in the universal "NO!" position. This physical boundary clearly tells the person you don't want him/her to come any closer. Keep your hands next to your face in case you need to protect your head (from a punch or slap, for example).

#2 Say no. If the person gets closer, extend your "NO!" hands forward a bit (as if to push the person back). Use a strong, assertive voice to say something like:

- "NO!" And if the person doesn't stop immediately, repeat: "I said NO!"

- "Leave me alone!"

- "Back off!"

- "Step away!"

- "I don't want to fight you, but I will if I have to." (Use this boundary only if you've taken a self-defense class.)

#3 Draw attention to yourself. If the person persists, yell to alert other people to the situation. You can shout:

- "I don't know this man!"

- "This person is bothering me!"

- "I want this guy to leave me alone!"

- "This girl is threatening me!"

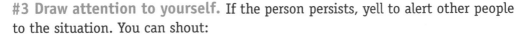

If the attacker gets into your physical space, keep your hands up to protect yourself and continue to yell in an assertive voice. If you feel it's safe to turn your back and run, then run to safety (go to a store, a group of people, an authority at school, a police/fire station, a security guard booth, or the home of a neighbor you know).

Whatever you do, especially if an attacker tries to grab you and stick you in a vehicle—*put up a fight.* Yell nonstop, kick, scratch, hit, kick him/her in the groin, poke the person's eyes. Do everything you can to avoid being taken somewhere else by a stranger or an abuser—give it everything you've got and then some. Studies show that you have less of a chance of surviving an attack alive if you're taken to a second location. Don't give up and don't stop yelling if that's what you have to do to survive or get free.

Street SMARTS

Being aware of your surroundings while you're out and about is another important part of defending yourself. Remember these tips, and you'll increase your safety. In all cases, trust your gut first and think later.

Walking. While in your neighborhood or around your community:

Do . . .

- ❖ Look around you and remain aware of your surroundings, including what's behind you.

- ❖ Walk assertively with purpose and look people in the eye as you pass them.

- ❖ Cross the street or change direction if someone walks too close or makes you uncomfortable. You can also go in a store or other public place for protection.

Don't . . .

✤ Walk with headphones on—you can't be fully aware of what's going on around you if you can't hear.

✤ Jabber away on a cell phone, which makes it hard to hear and see what's around you.

✤ Rely on stereotypes, like that well-dressed, good-looking people aren't dangerous.

✤ Worry about making someone feel bad if you turn around or cross the street. You have the right to feel safe, and that means taking precautions.

Hanging out. While you're having fun with friends, or if you're at a party where kids are drinking alcohol/doing drugs or where adults aren't present:

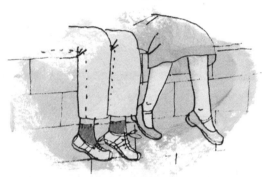

Do . . .

✤ Tell your parents or guardians where you'll be.

✤ Have a buddy system in place. You and your closest friend can make a pact to watch out for each other. If one of you wants to leave, then you both should leave together, no matter what.

✤ Have an alternative way to get home in case your ride falls through (or if the person who agreed to drive you home is no longer sober).

✤ Know what your boundaries are when it comes to smoking, drinking, or doing drugs (and stick to those boundaries).

SISTERHOOD

Girls need to stick together, so when it comes to self-defense, share your knowledge with other girls in your life and watch out for one another. Don't let a friend get into a car with a drunk driver or take off with a guy she just met (tell her why you're concerned and offer to help her find another way home). Even if you're not good friends with someone, don't let her do something she might regret or that could put her in harm's way. You have to watch each other's backs when it comes to real danger.

❧ Educate yourself about the most current date-rape drugs, which are designed to lower your defenses. Always get your own drink and keep your eye on it at all times to play it safe (date-rape drugs are usually slipped into drinks and don't have a taste).

Don't . . .

❧ Go to a party or event without planning how you're going to get home safely.

❧ Go into a room or secluded place (such as a mall parking lot or vacant school bleachers) with someone you just met, don't know that well, or who seems pushy.

❧ Allow someone you just met to hold or refill your glass or to open your drink while turned away from you.

Driving/riding. While you're on the go:

Do . . .

❧ Stay on high alert in parking lots and always walk with someone else, especially after dark.

❧ Request a security escort to your car if it's unsafe to walk alone. Places like malls, bus depots, or train stations usually have security escorts available.

❧ Look around to be aware of your surroundings—always move away from someone who makes you uncomfortable.

❧ Get into your car quickly and lock your door immediately after entering.

❧ Drive to a police/fire station, or a well-lit grocery store, if a stranger follows your car. Make a mental note of the vehicle's description and license number. Avoid driving home (so the person won't know where you live).

❧ Use a cell phone (if you have one) to call 911 or a parent if you're being followed. Make sure these numbers are programmed into the speed dial so you don't get into a car accident while trying to dial.

❧ Sit close to the bus/train driver when riding on public transportation. You'll be less likely to get harassed.

Don't . . .

❧ Walk to your car while you're talking on a cell phone—you won't be fully aware of what's going on around you.

❧ Go to your car if someone follows you—go where there are other people and report that you're being followed. Only enter your car as a last resort, if you're positive you can get in safely and quickly, and then lock the door. (Use your car's alarm/panic button if you have one.)

❧ Leave your windows or doors open/unlocked while you're in an isolated parking lot, because you're an easier target that way.

❧ Open your door or window for a stranger as you wait in your car. Keep the doors locked and have a cell phone handy, if possible, so you can call for help in an instant.

❧ Get into a car, bus, or elevator with someone who makes you uncomfortable.

❧ Hitchhike or pick up hitchhikers—ever.

Standing. While you're waiting for a bus or a ride, or you're just taking a rest somewhere:

Do . . .

❧ Look around and remain aware of your surroundings at all times.

❧ Stay with a group or with your friends—there's safety in numbers.

❧ Stand or sit assertively.

❧ Stay in a well-lit place if it's nighttime.

❧ Go somewhere safe, like a restaurant or gas station, if someone bothers you.

Don't . . .

❖ Stand where you can be cornered or pinned against a wall or structure—you need room to move and get away if someone bothers you.

❖ Get lost in a book or listen to loud music for long periods of time without looking up and around you.

❖ Allow someone you don't know to hang out with you if you're in an isolated area, such as a quiet corner of a park or an empty bus stop or station.

Check Out a
SELF-DEFENSE COURSE

No matter how assertive you are, some attackers won't stop. Or you might find yourself in a situation that's difficult to get out of (like you're with someone you trust who suddenly pins you down, or someone grabs you from behind). That's why it's so important to take a self-defense course created specifically for girls and women.

In a self-defense course, you'll learn actual fighting techniques that can help you feel stronger and safer. In fact, researchers have found that female graduates of self-defense courses experience higher self-confidence, have an increased ability to set boundaries, and enjoy more freedom in their everyday lives.[2]

Gut Check

Sometimes, people make up "poor me" or sympathy stories as a way to distract their victims, get something from them, or even harm them. (Like some people pretend that they lost a pet and might ask if they can see if it's in your backyard. Another common story is pretending to have car trouble.) Don't think that you have to pitch in and help a stranger if you don't feel safe. Trust your gut to determine whether you want to get involved. Think of alternative ways to help, like calling the police for the person or alerting an adult who can help.

Any self-defense fighting techniques class is better than no course at all. However, not all programs are created equal. Here are descriptions of self-defense courses that can help you learn to use your gut, boundaries, voice, and fighting techniques to defend yourself.

Martial arts: There are countless martial-arts combat methods that are usually practiced as a sport, including karate, kung fu, and tae kwon do.

Upside: You might be able to use some martial-arts moves to fight an attacker.

Downside: You'll learn a type of fighting that's somewhat choreographed and isn't always geared toward a female's strengths (or meant to be used to fight an assailant in a rape situation).

Impact self-defense (a.k.a. model mugging):
This method includes modified martial-arts and street-fight moves geared toward the strengths of the female body. Techniques are based on real-life scenarios gathered from police rape/assault reports and interviews with survivors and assailants. Fighting skills are practiced at full force on a model mugger in a classroom setting. The courses also cover how to deal with any emotional abuse (such as name-calling and threats) that an attacker might use.

Upside: You'll learn a real-world approach to self-defense, and your muscles can even memorize how to deliver blows that could knock out an assailant.

Downside: It may seem scary to fight an actual person and practice moves at 100 percent force, even though the model mugger is protected with gear.

Non-impact self-defense: Most courses offer information
about staying aware of your environment, setting boundaries effectively, and using your voice to protect yourself. The techniques are specifically geared toward girls and women. Some courses might also cover how to handle verbal abuse and the emotional aspects of an assault.

Upside: These courses are practical and beneficial because you'll learn how to protect yourself from an attack. Plus, it can be fun and empowering to participate in a class with other girls and women.

Downside: You don't get to practice self-defense moves at full force in a real fight.

SISTERHOOD

Taking a self-defense class with your friends can be fun and empowering. And if you've been hesitant to take one, you and a friend can support each other. Some schools will hire self-defense instructors to offer classes for physical education (P.E.) credit. Get together with your girlfriends and talk to your principal, P.E. teacher, or school nurse about offering a self-defense course at your school. Tell them why it's important to you and why you think many girls would benefit.

Self-defense books and videos: Most cover the same
information that's taught in a non-impact self-defense course.

Upside: You can pick up some basic tips, like how to set boundaries using your voice and how to be more aware of your surroundings. You can go at your own pace and practice the techniques whenever and wherever you like.

Downside: You won't have the benefit of a live instructor, who can tell you if you're practicing a technique correctly, or the camaraderie with other girls taking the class.

Before you sign up, be sure to interview the self-defense instructor to get the full scoop on what you'll learn. Ask questions like:

1. What will the focus of the class be (defense techniques, setting boundaries, conflict de-escalation)?

2. What is your background?

3. Will I learn some or all of the techniques at full force?

4. Will I learn any moves that are specific to getting out of rape situations?

5. Do you offer paid scholarships or payment plans for students with financial needs?

THE POWER OF SELF-DEFENSE

I'm glad I took a self-defense class. I feel better equipped to deal with unsafe situations I haven't experienced yet. I also feel stronger and safer when I'm alone.——Abby, 15

Now I'm way more aware of what's around me, and I'm watching who's watching me. Now I observe people's actions: the way they look at me, the way they walk, where they're going.——Summer, 13

When the model mugger walked out, my stomach flipped. In a way I felt embarrassed. But my classmates were supportive and said, "You can do it——you can keep going." I felt like my body was just taking over, and I was able to do all the things I had to do.——Faith, 13

My last fight in my impact self-defense class was such a big achievement. I felt way more powerful, like I was so strong and secure. When I was walking and the teacher came up from behind and "attacked" me, I felt like I knew what I was doing and I did——I knocked him out!——Zoe, 13

One weekend class is worth it to be able to defend yourself for the rest of your life.——Tanya, 15

reTroSPeCT:
YOUR EDUCATION RIGHTS

A girl didn't always have rights to an education in the United States. And even today, there are still struggles for those who are discriminated against to receive a fair and equal education. Now, after historical political battles, students who go to schools that receive federal funds or grants (and, in some cases, state funds) are required by law to receive an education that is harassment free and based on equality. Here are just some of the laws that aim to protect your rights:

Title VI of the Civil Rights Act of 1964. Prohibits discrimination based on race, color, or national origin in programs or activities receiving federal money, including schools.

Title IX of the Education Amendments of 1972. Prohibits discrimination based on sex in federally funded schools and programs. Protects all students from unlawful sexual harassment at school and during school-sponsored activities, limits single-sex education in coed schools to give girls the same opportunities as boys, and requires equal treatment, funding, and support for girls' athletics programs.

The Rehabilitation Act of 1973 and Americans with Disabilities Act (ADA) of 1990. These laws prohibit discrimination against persons with disabilities, requiring that they receive a quality education and have access to school buildings.

Sexual and gender identity laws. As of 2004, fewer than ten states have adopted laws to specifically protect gay, lesbian, bisexual, and transgender students from harassment or discrimination in public schools. To learn more, see: www.safeschoolscoalition.org.

11

Fighting for Your Rights at School

At best, school prepares you for life. You learn tons about the world and other people. You get to build skills, question the way things work, and think for yourself. You may love the scene—everything from your classes, to after-school activities, to hanging with your friends. But at its worst, school can be like a nightmare where hardly any learning happens because you're either bored out of your mind or busy trying to survive hostile hallways.

Many girls don't feel safe at school or while they're walking home or on the bus. They say that they're teased about their bodies, groped, or burned by the rumor of the week. Some girls are even tormented or beaten up by a bully or clique simply because of how they look, what they wear, where they come from, or what they like to do. And then there are girls who are more subtly held back: They learn little in class because the other students don't give them the respect they deserve, or they don't get the same educational opportunities that others do.

This isn't the way it's supposed to be! You have a right to an education that meets your needs, and you should always feel safe at school. Any form of harassment, such as bullying or discrimination, is a violation of your rights and, in many cases, the law. No matter what path you're on (and there are many) your education should help you become smarter, stronger, and more self-respecting. If this isn't the case, you can take action.

Taking control of your education includes facing what could be interfering with your learning. Like *Ms.* magazine cofounder and women's rights leader Gloria Steinem has said, "The first problem for all of us, both men and women, is not to learn but to *un*learn." What does she mean? For starters, that we all need to take a closer look at what stereotypes or unfair limitations may hold girls back in life—including what's limiting their rights at school.

Harassment AND Discrimination

The fact is 8 out of 10 students report that they experience some sort of sexual harassment at school.[1] If you're harassed at school, you may have scars (physical and emotional) that last long after graduation. If you're picked on or treated unfairly, you'll probably feel afraid at school, which interferes with your education. Girls who are harassed in one way or another are more likely to get lower grades or drop out. Research shows that victims can become depressed, lose sleep, develop eating disorders, get caught in an abusive cycle in their relationships, and more.

When you're not safe at school, you might feel like you don't count or have no power to stop the harassment. You *do* count. And you *can* take action to get the harassment-free, equal education you deserve.

Sometimes, harassment or discrimination might be really obvious to you, like when someone calls a student an insulting name. Other times, you might sense that something's wrong but not feel sure that it qualifies as harassment. Here's how to know these offenses when you see them, starting with their definitions:

Sexual harassment is . . .

Unwanted and unwelcome sexual attention, teasing, or touching. Harassment is more than a boy vs. girl issue. Both boys and girls can be harassed by someone of either sex, a group of kids, a teacher, or another adult. The U.S. Department of Education says that sexual harassment falls into two categories.

1. Hostile environment harassment: When the sexual harassment affects your right to your education, makes you afraid to go to school, prohibits you from participating in certain activities, or is abusive.

2. "Quid pro quo" harassment: When a school employee like a teacher or coach blackmails you (threatens to reveal something you want to hide) into doing a sexual act with him/her. Or he/she makes sexual advances in exchange for a higher grade or allowing you to participate in a school activity. The employee might threaten to fail you or to cut you from a team if you don't give in to the sexual demands—it's still harassment whether you say yes or no to the person.

All of the following activities are considered sexual harassment:

Taunts, such as sexual comments, jokes, or insults, based on anything from your sexual identity to your body type.

Looks or gestures, like a guy pretending to "get with" you from behind or simulating masturbation or oral sex in the halls or in class. Or being flashed, mooned, or spied on in the locker room at school as you dress or shower.

Rumors, like a sexual rumor that's spread by word of mouth, written on notes, bathroom walls, or yearbooks, or spread off campus through another student's Web site, email, or IMing. Being called a "slut" is a sexual rumor, too.

Exposure to explicit images, like if students are looking at a porn magazine and you see it over their shoulders.

Unwanted touching or physical contact, such as fondling, pinching, grabbing, or rubbing. Other unwanted contact may include having your clothes tugged or torn off, being forced to touch, hug, or kiss someone, or being cornered or restrained in a sexually threatening way.

Bullying is . . .

Intimidating, threatening, or harming a classmate. Sexual harassment is just one tactic bullies use to try to gain power over their victims and to mentally and physically abuse classmates. Bullies are aggressive. They push others around, tease, or assault classmates (kicking, punching, shoving, slapping, tripping, and so on). Sometimes, bullies will even victimize their own friends by stealing their money or belongings, threatening them through fear of rejection, or retaliation, or turning a group of friends against them.

> My friend was being harassed by a group of guys in her class. They would always talk dirty to her and make her uncomfortable. It went on the whole school year, right in front of the teacher.
> —Daisy, 15

My friend is gay and he's been called a "fag" in the hallways, which is something our Gay Student Association is trying to end at our school.—Jennifer, 15

At my school, the guy basketball players are treated like gods who are sponsored by major companies and get lots of free shoes and jerseys. The girls' team gets nothing, but we try just as hard as they do.
—Holly, 14

Discrimination is . . .

Being treated unequally based on your race, color, sex, religion, sexual identity, national origin, or disabilities. If you're not getting the education you deserve because of one of the "-isms" (page 9) like sexism or racism, that's discrimination and is prohibited in schools that receive federal funding. Whether the discrimination is coming from students, teachers, school officials, or parents on campus, it's wrong. Discrimination can include students calling others racist names or picking on students who are disabled or from other countries. Another form of discrimination occurs when a school doesn't equally fund activities for girls and boys.

Standing UP

So, is your school a place where everyone is treated equally? Sometimes, discrimination goes on so quietly that no one notices. To get in touch with what's happening at your school, spend a day watching people, investigating, and taking notes. What you discover might inspire you to come up with a plan for spreading more respect at your school.

If your school receives *any* federal funds (or, in some cases, state funds), then it is required by law to have a sexual harassment policy and to enforce it. Many girls don't report harassment because they assume it's not a big deal, don't want to make it worse, or don't think anyone will care. But your education is vital to your self-respect and your future success—and you can fight for it.

One teacher always calls girls up to the board and looks at us from head to toe. He told me I looked like his girlfriend from college, which made me feel weird.—Mayra, 14

Ending harassment starts by saying it's wrong and deciding to do something about it. Here's what you can do, whether your school has a policy in place or not:

1. Set a Boundary

Most harassers and bullies expect their victims to keep their mouths shut. When harassers say something lewd or rude, you could ignore them so you're not giving them the reaction they want (you still can report the harassment, even if it occurred only once). Or you could set a boundary by speaking up.

First, check your gut to decide if it's safe to stand up to the harasser(s). Make sure you feel secure before you say anything and remember that the goal is to de-escalate a situation, instead of making it worse. (See Chapter 10 to learn more about safety tips, how to say no with power, and what standing strong and confident looks like.) Here's what you could say in some common situations:

Situation: You're called a "slut," "ho," "bitch," or some other degrading name by another student.

Try: "Please don't call me that again—it's disrespectful. I'll report you if you do it again." And you can add, "Plus, it's against our school's anti-harassment policy."

Situation: When you walk down the hall at school, a guy says he wants to (fill in the rude sexual act) to you.

Try: Ignoring him. Or, if you feel safe, speak up right then or pull him aside later when he's away from his friends. You might say, "What you said to me was really disrespectful. Did you know sexual harassment is against school rules? I want you to stop, and I'll report you if you don't."

Situation: The leader of a group of girls (who could be your friends or not) cuts you down or tries to embarrass you when you walk by the group.

Try: Asking her if you can speak with her alone. Or, if you feel confident, approach her in front of the group and say, "I'd like you to stop making fun of me. It hurts my feelings. I'm not sure why you're doing it—but it's not cool and it has to stop." If you've already asked her to stop and she continues, give her a warning like, "I've already asked you to stop. I'll have to report you if this happens again."

Situation: During class, another student threatens to hurt you in some way after school.

Try: Looking the person in the eye and saying, "I don't want to fight you. If you want to talk about something with me—or if I've done something to offend you—then we can do that when you calm down. But I'm not going to fight you." If you feel threatened, seek help from an adult immediately, and report the incident to your school.

Situation: A guy at school grabs your rear end, snaps your bra, or sandwiches you between him and a friend.

Try: Putting your hands up in front of your chest (as if pushing the guy away) and saying, "Stop it!" in a loud, firm voice. In a situation like this, it's best to report the incident immediately. Be sure to follow through with the next step, which is documenting what happened so you have a written record.

2. Document It

You may have been told that it's not OK to "tattle," but harassment is a major violation of your rights and needs to be stopped so you can get a good education and reach your full potential. If harassment is going down, act like a news reporter and get the facts. Before you file a complaint, write down the "four Ws" of the incident(s): who, where, when, what. To keep the facts straight, document the incident immediately after it takes place.

Who is the harasser/bully? Write down the first and last name of the offender, if possible. Or be able to describe him/her really well (such as who the person hangs around with, classes he/she is in, or what the person looks like). Note the names of any witnesses or accomplices.

Where did it occur? Location is important, especially if it happened on school grounds or during school hours but off campus (like on the bus or during an event at another local school). Even if the incident took place off school grounds, you can still file a report if you and the harasser go to the same school. If the incident happened in class, write down the name of the class and the teacher.

When did it occur? Write the date and time of the incident(s).

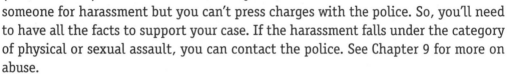

What happened? Document step by step, word for word, what took place. Just stick to the facts of what happened (as if you had recorded the incident on video and are now playing it back from start to finish), so you can accurately report it.

Documentation is essential when it comes to sexual harassment because it is considered a civil (not a criminal) violation, which means you can sue someone for harassment but you can't press charges with the police. So, you'll need to have all the facts to support your case. If the harassment falls under the category of physical or sexual assault, you can contact the police. See Chapter 9 for more on abuse.

3. Report It

Many harassers threaten revenge if you tell on them. While some mean it, many just hand out empty threats or may try to bully you into pretending nothing happened. Check your gut and decide what's best for you—do you want to report the incident? Remember, if you don't stand up to harassment, then you (and other girls) are being hurt not only by the harasser but also by the injustice of the situation. Even if you're scared, telling someone what happened is the right thing to do. Try these tips for handling the situation:

Know who you can trust. Create a support network of adults or family members who can help protect you. Tell them what's going on and how it's affecting you. Ask for help in filing a complaint with your school.

Know your rights. Get to know your school's sexual harassment policy and complaint process by asking the main office for a copy of the policy. If your school doesn't have a policy, ask about the general process for filing a complaint. Note: You might have to follow specific steps, depending on your school's policy. If your school doesn't have a policy, see "The New School Spirit" on page 181. If you go to a private or religious school that doesn't receive federal money, contact the National Women's Law Center (see page 218) for advice about how you can take action.

Know who to tell. If you go to a school that receives federal funds, the policy should include the name of your school's Title IX coordinator. (Every school or district is supposed to appoint an employee who's responsible for handling complaints properly.) If your school doesn't have a Title IX coordinator, go to your principal or dean of students for help.

Know your four Ws. Using the details you documented about the incident(s), you can draft your official complaint or explain the incident in a meeting with a school official.

Know the process. Ask what steps the school has taken to notify all the students of its harassment policy and procedure. When a complaint is filed, your school should immediately take steps to stop the harassment and prevent it from happening again (even if you go to a religious or private school with no policy, you still have a right to feel safe). If you don't want your name to be used, find out if your complaint can be kept confidential before you give any details.

Know what's being done. Don't just file your complaint and forget about it. Stay on top of the problem, especially if the harassment or bullying hasn't stopped or has gotten worse. Within a week of the complaint—or sooner if another incident has occurred—set up a meeting with the appropriate school official. In follow-up meetings, make sure to provide documentation of any new incidents. Bring a notepad and, if possible, ask a parent or guardian to attend the meeting with you. Document what your school official says and what promises are made.

Questions you can ask:

- What happened to the offender?

- What's being done to make sure the behavior stops and that I'm safe?

- What should I do if it happens again?

- What is the school doing overall to end harassment and bullying?

- When can we meet again? (Schedule a follow-up meeting within a week.)

Know your options. By your second follow-up meeting, if you're not satisfied with how your complaint is being handled, you still don't feel safe, or the harassment has continued, get help from a higher authority. You can always complain to your school official's supervisor or boss. Here's what to do:

%% Ask the school official who his/her supervisor is. If you've been dealing with your principal, his/her boss might be the school board or school superintendent. You can get the superintendent's number from your school secretary or the phone book (look for your school district's name).

%% Immediately schedule a meeting about your case with the supervisor. Bring your original documentation about the incident(s) of harassment or discrimination, as well as the documentation from your meetings with your school official.

%% Invite your school official to the meeting. This person can still help work on a solution, even if he/she hasn't been effective in the past.

%% Follow the same documentation procedures and follow-up steps with the supervisor.

4. Take It to the Next Level

If speaking up and filing a complaint with various school officials hasn't helped, don't give up. Instead, call in the government. You can file a complaint with the U.S. Department of Education: Office for Civil Rights (OCR), which enforces certain laws at your school. The OCR will review your complaint and then advise you on the next steps to take, which can sometimes include filing a federal lawsuit against your school and/or the offenders. See page 218 for how to contact the OCR and where to file your complaint. If the OCR can't help you and the harassment or discrimination still hasn't stopped, then you can talk to your parents or guardians about seeking outside legal advice, such as contacting the American Civil Liberties Union (see page 210).

FYI: Working Girls

Teen girls are a huge part of the workforce, making money through after-school jobs at restaurants, grocery stores, movie theaters, fast-food chains, and more. But they're now also part of a growing number of sexual harassment cases filed against employers, according to the U.S. Equal Employment Opportunity Commission (EEOC), which enforces federal laws prohibiting employment discrimination. Some girls have even been granted large settlements by well-known companies (meaning the businesses agreed to pay fines).

How do you recognize unlawful harassment in the workplace? It may include coworkers or a supervisor talking dirty or making lewd comments, telling sexist jokes, exposing you to sexual images, or hitting on you. If you're paid less than your male coworkers for doing the same job, that could be considered discrimination. If this has happened to you, try these steps:

❧ Complain to your supervisor or to corporate headquarters. If the harassment doesn't stop or if you've been retaliated against after reporting it to your employer, you can file a complaint with the EEOC.

❧ File a formal job discrimination complaint with the EEOC called a "Charge of Discrimination." This complaint has to be filed before you can pursue a job-discrimination lawsuit against your employer. There are strict time limits for filing a complaint with the EEOC, so act fast.

❧ Wait to learn whether your complaint will be investigated or dismissed. If the EEOC administrative judge finds that discrimination took place, he/she then decides how to remedy the situation and, in some cases, how you'll be compensated for the harm done. Go to the EEOC Youth at Work site to find out more about how to file a complaint (see page 218).

STOP the Rumor Mill

Of all the ways in which students are harassed, 75 percent of them (boys included) say they're most upset when the harassment involves a sexual rumor about them.[2] For girls, this usually means being called a name like "slut" or "ho." A girl can become the victim of a sexual rumor for any reason, from being different to being a victim of someone who wants easy revenge. Rumor-slingers know that spreading the word that a girl is a slut can damage her reputation.

If you're a girl who's caught in the rumor mill, here's how to tear it down:

SISTERHOOD

When girls call each other "sluts" or "hos" in the hallways or after school, they're doing even more harm than they realize. They're hurting not only their victim but also *themselves* by sending the message that it's OK to disrespect girls. The next time you hear someone using these words to slam another girl, challenge the person by speaking up—and show that you care about yourself, other girls, and sisterhood.

Go to the source. If you know who started the rumor(s), try talking to the person alone and in a safe place. Don't yell or make accusations—tell the insult-slinger how the rumor makes you feel and ask him/her to stop.

Get help. Depending on the outcome, you also might tell a school counselor, a teacher, or your school's Title IX coordinator. If the rumors get worse, the school official will be able to stand behind you as a witness to the harassment. Tell a parent or trusted adult what's going on so they can back you up.

Believe in yourself. Stay focused on what your education means to you—don't let a rumor derail you from your goals. At school, hang with friends who know the real you and will support you. Ask them to stand up on your behalf.

Come clean. Have you ever spread rumors, bullied someone, or even threatened another student in some way? (You wouldn't be the first.) Your education is about growing into a smarter, more self-respecting girl—so ask yourself how you can make changes for the better. For example, if you've spread a rumor, you could apologize to the girl you've hurt, especially if she was a friend. Make a promise to yourself not to bully or bash other girls anymore.

Girl Fights

More and more girls say that girl fights are happening in their schools—which goes against the idea of sisterhood and makes school a more dangerous place to be. When a girl picks a fight, it could be a sign that she feels powerless in her life (so she bullies others to feel in control). Or maybe she's gotten a reputation for being tough or good at fighting, and so it almost feels like an accomplishment to her. Or maybe she's learned that the only way to protect herself from being jumped at school is to start fights first.

> A girl called me a "dirty Mexican," and her friends circled me and jumped me.
> —Maria, 14

If you're the one starting fights, you probably know deep down that hurting other girls doesn't feel good. And if you mess with the wrong person, you might face some serious consequences, like getting beaten up or even getting in trouble with the police. Ask yourself what's really going on. Are you trying to fight for respect by using your fists? Do you have family problems that you don't know how to handle? Have you been abused and feel powerless? (See Chapter 9, which covers abuse and getting help.)

If you're sick of girls fighting at your school or if you've been in fights before, here are some do's and don'ts to help stop the violence and rebuild respect:

Do . . .

❧ Ask for help in dealing with your feelings and aggression, and making things right with the people you've hurt.

❧ Use communication to resolve arguments or misunderstandings.

❧ Document and report being threatened or physically assaulted by another student.

❧ Talk to other girls at your school about why girls fight and how you can work together to stop the violence.

Don't . . .

❧ Encourage other girls to fight.

❧ Watch fights for entertainment.

❧ Stand on the sidelines during a fight—quickly get an adult to help break it up.

❧ Start fights yourself (think about why you find it difficult to control your anger and how you can make changes for the better).

Pick Your Brain

In your journal, write about any roadblocks to your education and how you've been successful in the past. Think about ways to let self-respect rule your schooling.

I've felt held back in the past because: _____

I feel safe/unsafe at school when: _____

My family supports/discourages my education by: _____

I learn best in school when: _____

I'd like to explore the following interests outside of school:_____

My education goals are: _____

I'm making the most of school and will reach my goals by:_____

The NEW School SPIRIT

If you don't want to sit back while girls are held back, harassed, or discriminated against at your school, you can start a campaign to spread respect. Sometimes, all it takes is the leadership and vision of one person to get people thinking in a different way. That's how social activism starts—usually with an individual who has a dream for a better world and a plan to back it up. To make your school safer and more supportive for all girls:

> I speak my mind in class—girls' opinions are important and should be heard.
> —Caterina 16

Band together. If you need more challenges or are struggling in your classes, get together with other girls to start a study group. You can do your homework together, have lively discussions, and build sisterhood along the way. You can even take this idea a step further by starting a tutoring center at your school. Talk to your guidance counselor or principal about recruiting college students (who might get school credit or want to be teachers someday) to tutor you and other girls in certain classes or areas of interest. Of course, you can invite boys to participate, too—one more way to spread equality and respect.

Be seen and heard. Some girls struggle through school without ever raising their hand. Remember: You are worthy of a stellar education, and you do belong. If you're not doing well in certain classes, talk to your guidance counselor about receiving extra support, like changing your schedule or meeting with your teachers to find ways to get back on track. If you get a poor grade or need more feedback on an assignment, empower yourself by talking to the teacher about what you can do next. Grades aren't supposed to be an assessment of your character—they're a mark of your progress and where you can improve. To build up your confidence, talk with your teachers and contribute in class discussions. If you make this a habit, it'll be easier for you to speak up and express your views not only in class but all of the time. **Your opinion matters!**

Teach respect. Take a closer look at what's being taught at your school about social equality, acceptance, and tolerance. Is there room to add more respect-based topics to the lineup? Check out local college course catalogs and come up with a suggestion for new lessons that could be added to your current classes. (Many colleges offer courses in women's studies, ethnic studies, or human rights, for example.) Work with your teachers to put together a recommended list of books and movies that have themes of tolerance and equality. See if your school librarian might want help with setting up a special resources section to educate students about past and current campaigns for human rights. You can even offer your ideas before the school board, which usually plays a big role in making decisions about curriculum.

Talk with teachers. Some girls say they see disrespect going on in class behind the teacher's back (like other students making nasty gestures or bullying), but they don't want to tell on anyone. Your teachers can be your greatest allies in spreading respect, so let them know what's going on. Set up a meeting with your teachers after school to talk about the harassment. See if they might remind the students of your school's anti-harassment policy, either in class or during an assembly. If you feel that a teacher is doing something disrespectful, like treating guys and girls differently or ignoring student harassment, talk to him/her about the situation. You may decide to get the principal involved, too.

Draft a respect contract. Talk to your teachers about creating a "Respect Contract." You and the other students can brainstorm to decide what respect means, how you'll show each other respect in class, and what will happen if someone violates the contract (including the teacher). For example, that person might have to formally apologize to the class. The contract should be clearly written, signed, and posted for all to read. If you feel like your entire school needs to get with the program, talk to your principal about creating a contract that all of the students sign.

Raise awareness. If your school hasn't done much—or anything at all—to publicize its harassment policy, talk to your principal about holding an assembly to spread the word. If your school doesn't have a policy, it should (and you can tell your principal why).

My high school encourages young women to lead locally and in the world. We have special supervised activities, like learning what it's like to be homeless for a weekend by going to a homeless shelter and actually living on the street. We have to volunteer, and we take classes like "Social Justice" and "Global Women's Issues."
—Farah, 16

When people are disruptive in class, my teacher makes the student write an apology letter to the class and read it aloud. It makes me feel like our teacher really cares.
—Jodi, 15

SPeak UP

If you've done your best to fight harassment and bullying at school but you still feel victimized, it may be time to try an alternative route. Changing schools could be a last resort, and you'll need to discuss it with your parents or guardians first. Maybe you'd learn better at an alternative school, in an all-girl environment, or at a magnet school (in which you spend more of your day focusing on a topic you really love, like science or foreign languages). Another option is to become an independent study student, which is similar to being homeschooled, except you still meet with your teachers for support, discussions, and testing.

Push for changes. If you think your school board needs to pass a stronger sexual harassment or anti-discrimination policy, start by organizing. Follow these steps that other girls have used to get their schools to adopt policies:

- Talk to your friends about getting together to make a change.

- Get parents involved in your efforts.

- Talk to your principal about what you want to do. Find out how he/she can help.

- Use resources such as the National Women's Law Center (see page 218) to get help drafting your policy and to learn how your school can adopt it.

- Make the policy easy for students to understand, such as using a Q&A format that explains harassment and discrimination, who to go to for help, what happens during the complaint process, how offenders will be disciplined, and how students can prevent future harassment and discrimination.

- Talk to school board members and go to their meetings so that when your policy comes before them for approval they'll know who you are and will listen to your POV.

My Say

How Girls Fought to End Sexual Harassment

When Brenda Ramirez was 15, she joined the Young Women's Project (YWP), an organization that develops teen girls into leaders who can transform their communities. Soon after, Brenda joined a YWP effort, known as "The Sexual Harassment Campaign," to spread more respect and safety in Washington, D.C., schools.

On why she took action:

"I saw sexual harassment throughout elementary school, junior high, and high school. I saw things that most kids didn't consider harassment, like verbal bullying or guys touching girls in inappropriate ways. Girls would do it, too. It was like it was 'normal' because nothing was done about it. But in some cases, girls tried to avoid going to class or would avoid certain routes to class. Harassment invades your space and interferes with your education. It's your right to be able to go to class and concentrate."

On her goals and mission:

"Part of the problem was that D.C. public schools didn't have a consistent sexual harassment policy. Instead, the district had a directive that was drafted by the school district's superintendent. The trouble was, each time the superintendent changed, so did the sexual harassment directive—kids didn't know the rules when it came to sexual harassment, and the rules kept changing. We wanted the school district to pass a single policy that every school would follow and publicize.

"We learned about how the school board made decisions, and how policies are adopted in the school district. We organized meetings to get community support and surveyed students about their experiences with sexual harassment. Then we worked with the National Women's Law Center to draft a new policy, along with a user-friendly version for students. We had to testify before the school district two times, which required preparation and learning about public speaking. Our campaign was a success: The policy was passed by the school board in 2002."

On the changes that came about:

"Now, D.C. students can learn what sexual harassment is and how to deal with it. We even oversaw classroom training about the policy for 1,600 students. It's inspiring to see that you can start a project like ours, work together, and bring about social change. Girls can help improve their schools."

Girls For A CHANGE

As a college student, Whitney Smith learned that she could make a difference for herself and other young women by taking action. Once she graduated, she decided to teach leadership skills to teen girls in her community. In 2000, Whitney founded Girls For A Change (GFC), a nonprofit organization that matches female coaches with teams of girls who work together to identify a social problem, get to its root cause, and design a project to address the problem and make a lasting change. Here are just some of the issues GFC teams have tackled:

Improving girls' body image:

A team of middle school girls noticed that a lot of female students were dressing to get boys' attention or to mimic images they saw in the media. The GFC team decided to work with body-image experts who conducted workshops to teach girls that feeling good on the inside is what really counts.

Breaking down stereotypes:

Another GFC team is creating a newsletter for girls to break down traditional female stereotypes (like that girls can't do certain jobs that guys can do). The team will write feature stories about powerful women in their community as a way to promote strong female role models.

Supporting little sisters:

When a group of high school girls involved in GFC wanted to help younger girls in their community, they raised almost $2,000 to run a weekly after-school program that offers confidence-boosting activities like dance, art, and sports.

These girls are making a change, and so can you! To learn more about Girls For A Change, see page 218.

12

Spreading Respect

Throughout history, women and girls around the world have bravely fought for respect—taking both small and gigantic risks—so that females everywhere could live more freely, safely, and equally. The fight for your rights is still on and needs your support. Every girl can be a respect activist in her home, school hallways, community, and around the world. Taking action to break down barriers is more than a choice for girls—it's a necessity. You have to protect your rights and keep pushing past limitations, on behalf of girls everywhere.

To make a difference, you don't have to be an adult, a politician, professionally experienced, or backed by tons of money. The way you live your life—trusting your gut, standing up for yourself, and being the real you—makes the world a better place because you set an example that can teach people everywhere how to treat girls with respect. If girls like you take action, the changes you make (starting with the changes in yourself) cause a positive ripple effect that can touch the lives of all girls. And this is the real nature of sisterhood.

It's seeing yourself in other girls, caring about them, supporting their efforts, and wanting them to have what you should always want for yourself: respect.

Girl on a MISSION

Part of spreading respect is being a girl on a mission. You find your mission by keeping your eyes wide open. When you see a problem, take notice. Imagine what you can do about it. Then take a stand by speaking your mind. Here's how:

❧ Write a letter to a company if you find fault with its products or practices. Express your opinion and suggest changes.

❧ Send an email or letter to your congressperson to fight a law that's unjust or lobby for legislation to better protect girls' rights.

❧ Call a meeting with your principal to discuss disrespectful behavior going on at school, what needs to change, and how you might help.

❧ Speak up if you've been sexually harassed, bullied, or abused, or if other girls you know have been harmed by violence. Seek the help of adults you trust or start by calling a crisis helpline.

❧ Write an editorial for your school or local newspaper about a problem in your community (like if funding has been cut for girls' after-school programs). Or contact reporters who have written articles about related topics and suggest they explore the problem further.

❧ Create artwork, poems, stories, or essays that express your views about what's happening to girls in your community or the world. You might even sell your work to raise money for a cause that supports girls.

❧ Give a speech at school, attend a local political event, or run for student government to spread the word about respect or other causes you care about.

I volunteer for various girls' centers. One of them provides two-week-long hiking trips where urban teen girls are taught courage, feminism, teamwork, and self-respect.
—Rachel, 18

I wrote an editorial about a school assembly skit that was offensive to gays and lesbians. When my vice principal tried to censor my editorial, I met with him to discuss it and he came to see my point of view. The article got people talking.—Cara, 17

Get INVOLVED

Taking action doesn't have to be a solo effort—if you want, you can join with others. What's your mission . . . saving the environment? Improving education? Fighting crime? Lobbying for better healthcare for women and children? Ending human rights violations? You can probably find a local or national organization that's fighting for the same cause.

I volunteer with an organization that helps children get out of sweatshops and get back into school.
—Sasha, 18

Find a match. Do a quick search on the Internet, flip through the phone book, or ask people you know for their recommendations. Every nonprofit organization has a mission statement, so make sure to read up on the history, goals, founders, funding sources, and past accomplishments (or possible scandals). Learn all you can about the organization you choose and see if you agree with its position and mission.

Make contact. Call or email the organization to ask how you can get involved. (Can you volunteer? Sign a petition? Organize others in your neighborhood?) Tip: Think about talking to the adults in your family about your plans. They'll probably feel more comfortable if the organization is well established and has a central meeting place and designated leader they can check out.

Figure out your role. Activism can be hard work, but it should also give you a sense of accomplishment. So once you get involved with a group, make sure to speak up about your talents and how you can contribute. For example, if you love to write, you might be able to help with a letter-writing campaign vs. just stuffing envelopes.

Make the most of it. Listen to what other group members have to say, but don't be afraid to pitch your own ideas. Speak up if you feel like the meetings aren't productive or if the group isn't making progress.

See how it's going. After a few weeks of participation, do a progress check. Do you feel like the group is accomplishing significant goals? Do you enjoy your work there? Your time and power should be well spent—but if they're not, you don't have to stick around. You might make more of a difference with another group or by taking the lead.

CHANGE Your World

Heading up an effort to make a difference can strengthen your self-respect in so many ways: You'll feel like you have a purpose. You'll tap into your creativity and power. You'll figure out how to make decisions and motivate people. And you'll find out what you're made of (and what you still need to learn).

Identify the Problem and Your Allies

To make changes, you first have to focus on a specific problem and come up with solutions. Are you fired up about how girls are disrespected in your school's hallways? Do you see examples of girls not having equal rights? Are girls being harmed or victimized in your community? Start small by choosing one issue—you can't change the world overnight! Think about how the issue affects you personally or what it means to other girls.

> I joined a program to learn how to make public service announcements and documentaries, so I can show other girls that the real world is not the "perfect" world they see in the media.
> —Tina, 15

Once you know what the problem is, you're ready to take the next step: getting other people to see it, too. Finding allies is about inspiring people to be on your side. How do you find them? Just look around you.

Who do you know? Think about everyone you know who's being hurt or affected by the problem you've identified, including girls, guys, or adults (parents, teachers, community leaders, and so on). Look for groups that are already working on the same issue—ask if you can use their research, pick their brains, or join forces.

Why should they care? People will be more interested and invested if they can personally relate to the issue. So, come up with reasons to convince them to support your cause. The best way to get people on your side is to approach them positively. Explain who you are, your cause, why it matters, and how they can help. Remember that they're probably thinking, "Why should this matter to me?" Have your answers ready.

Get Organized

Once you've made your list of allies and convinced them to join you, you need to bring your group together so you can create a plan of action. Here's how to start:

Find a central meeting place. Ask your principal for access to a classroom, gather at your home (if a parent says it's OK), or meet at a local park, plaza, library, or community center.

Pick a time. Try to choose a time that works best for most of the group. People who are really inspired will find time to be a part of your mission. Tip: Bring some drinks and snacks to share so everyone will be energized.

Set an agenda. Before the meeting, write up an agenda or to-do list so the group can stay on track. Include each part of the meeting: introductions, a recap of the problem you've identified, discussion topics, and time for questions afterward. Don't let the meeting run too long. When people start to look tired, wrap it up. At the next meeting, you can continue where you left off.

Make introductions. Do people in the group know each other already? If not, ask everyone to introduce themselves and talk about why they decided to get involved. Or try the Interview Game: Divide people into pairs, have them interview each other for a few minutes, and then ask each person to tell the group about who they interviewed.

Set some standards. Decide as a group how each meeting will work. For example, the first few minutes can be spent catching up or introducing new members, and the rest of the time can be reserved for action items. Agree on some rules for respectful communication: How will you give everyone a chance to talk? Will you make decisions by majority vote?

Plan the next steps. At the end of the first meeting, ask for volunteers to help prepare the next meeting's agenda. Consider using an email list to stay in touch between meetings.

Talk Solutions

When you explore solutions in a group, there's strength in numbers—you'll have more ideas, more points of view, and more voices. Use the meeting to get

As part of a social change project, other girls and I created a video to encourage teens to get out and volunteer with organizations like a food bank and shelter in our area.—Larissa, 16

yourselves fired up about making positive changes. Have a brainstorming session, which works like this:

Share ideas. On a chalkboard or a big sheet of paper hanging on the wall, write one sentence that describes the problem. Ask the group to share ideas about the possible cause(s) of the problem, and appoint someone to jot down the ideas on the board/paper. A good way to go from talking about the problem to finding its root cause is to keep asking *why* until you hit on something concrete. (For example: Problem—Many girls don't respect each other at school. Why? Maybe they feel competitive with each other. Why? They feel insecure. Why? They need to learn to be more confident in who they are. Bingo!) Remind people that brainstorming is the fun part and that any idea is worth bringing up—you'll analyze the ideas later to see what's realistic.

Pinpoint reasons. Which idea/reason seems to be the most likely source of the problem your group has identified? Sometimes, issues are so complex that you can't find only one reason, but try to focus on no more than two, if possible.

Settle on a solution. Now that you've identified a reason for the problem, how might you help solve it or address it? Start the brainstorming process again. Come up with one or two specific solutions that the group agrees could have the greatest impact.

Come Up with a Plan

So, how can you turn your solution into a "campaign" (an organized effort to make a change)? At your next meeting, start creating a plan of action. In a notebook or on a computer, keep an ongoing list using each of the bold/blue items on these two pages—these are the essential parts of your plan. Then leave space to fill in each item.

Research: What's the best way to get more informed about the problem and your potential solution? Research. Your group can sift through news reports, conduct interviews with experts, or put together a local, school, or Web-based survey. Another option is to meet with a company, a nonprofit organization, or another group that's knowledgeable about the issue.

Who: Decide who your audience is (students, community members, lawmakers).

What: What's the best way to reach or educate this audience? Through the written word? By staging an event?

How: *How* will you do it? Think of this as your campaign.

Campaign strategies to consider:

❧ **Get the word out.** Make fliers, pamphlets, or posters. Start an email campaign. See if you can educate people through a radio program or the TV news. Or start your own media outlet, such as a magazine or Web site (see "Take Back the Media" on page 60 for ideas).

❧ **Get people together and talking.** Events such as assemblies, workshops, health fairs, or summits can combat a problem through education. Your event could sponsor discussions and debates, where girls and their advocates get the chance to speak out.

❧ **Get out on the streets or take the stage.** Your campaign might take shape as a rally, march, boycott, protest, concert, sporting event, play, exhibit, or presentation. Or your event might combine raising money with raising awareness.

> My friends and I participated in an AIDS Walk fundraiser because we learned that more and more teens are getting infected with HIV. We felt like we were a part of helping to save people's lives.
> —Angie, 14

Supporters: Do you need experts or decision-makers to help you carry out your plans? For example, if you want to do something at school, do you need to involve the principal or a teacher? Talk to adults who can help you.

Costs: Do parts of the campaign cost money—and if so, how will you raise those funds? A bake sale? Car wash? Donations?

Tasks and timeline: What do you need to do to achieve the goals you've set? Identify each task, and then ask for volunteers for each one. Create a timeline from start to finish and include all the tasks that need to be completed. Set a deadline for each task.

Bring your list to every meeting and revise it as needed. Review the tasks—have they been completed? Have new ones come up? Do you need more volunteers? Take a look at the timeline—are you on schedule? Do you need to tweak your deadlines? What's working and what's not? You may have to change parts of the action plan or find new ways to reach your goals. No plan is perfect from the start.

GIRLS IN ACTION

When a group of high school girls saw their friends become victims of violence in their community, they didn't just get mad—they got involved. They came up with a plan to educate girls about violence and abuse, getting help, and supporting a friend who's been hurt. Here, the girls share how they're working together:

"We meet one day a week at a local community center in our neighborhood where we hang out after school. During some of our first meetings, we talked about how girls are often victims of violence or abuse and how we could help. We thought that girls in our community needed to be educated about the different kinds of abuse—from emotional, to physical, to sexual—so they could learn how to protect themselves or get help. We brainstormed a list of ideas and invited experts to our meetings so we could learn more."

 Ideas:

★ Hand out fliers around our neighborhood and school describing types of abuse and how to get help.

★ Organize a self-defense class at the community center.

★ Invite a speaker to come to our school to talk about violence against girls and how to stop it.

"We spent a few meetings talking about each idea and took a vote to decide which solution we'd turn into our campaign for change. We decided to make fliers and organize an assembly at our school, and then we came up with our plan."

The Plan:

RESEARCH: Find out about the types of abuse and violence against girls, get numbers of crisis helplines, and gather tips from crime-prevention organizations.

WHO: We want to distribute the fliers to girls in our community and at school. The assembly will be for all students at our school.

HOW: We'll create a flier that gives descriptions of different kinds of abuse. We'll list 24-hour crisis helplines and give tips for how to help a friend who's been a victim. The assembly guest speaker will talk about what students can do to stop violence and get help.

SUPPORTERS: School principal (to help set up assembly). Parents (to help design the flier). Community center director (to refer us to speakers and resources). Librarian (for help with research). Speaker (we need someone who will do it for free). Volunteers (to pass out fliers in our neighborhood).

COSTS: We need money to print the fliers and we can ask our school to help.

The Tasks:

⭐ Talk to principal, set date for assembly.

⭐ Find and confirm speaker.

⭐ Write and design the flier, and then print it.

⭐ Find volunteers to help with plan.

⭐ Hand out fliers.

⭐ Make posters to hang at school for the assembly.

⭐ Hold assembly.

⭐ Send thank-you card to speaker and principal.

"Finally, we decided on how we'd celebrate once our project was complete. We plan to go out for pizza with all the people who are helping us and with our parents. We have even promised to pay!"

Make Your Voice HEARD

Whether you're on a one-girl mission or you're leading a movement to get more respect for girls, you have a constitutional right to speak your mind. Freedom of speech is what makes activism, organizing, and campaigning possible. Here are some ways to speak up and speak out:

Write a Call-to-Action Letter

Writing to decision-makers is a smart way to take action. To really turn up the heat, get your allies involved in your letter-writing campaign. You can either come up with a form letter that you each sign individually (you can have everyone personalize their letter in some way first) or write one letter that you have everyone sign.

1   Make sure names and addresses are correct.

2   Always start letters with "Dear Ms./Mr./Mrs." and the person's last name.

3   Your introduction can include an example, statistic, or testimonial that describes the problem and grabs the decision-maker's attention. (Giving real examples is stronger and more effective than just venting.) Try to include details like how long the problem has been going on and examples of the harm being done.

4   Describe how the problem affects you and other girls. Strengthen your position using facts or statistics. Also, describe the root cause of the problem and what you've tried to do about it, if applicable.

5   Give clear reasons why you want the decision-maker to get involved. You might even suggest some steps you could take by working *together*.

6   Restate the urgency of the situation or your campaign. Close your letter in a strong but polite way, and request a meeting to get faster results or move things forward.

Here's an example:

Your Name
Address
City, State ZIP

Date

Decision-Maker's Name
Title
Address
City, State ZIP

Dear Ms. (Last Name),

For the past year, school has been a nightmare for me. Almost every day a group of girls in my grade has called me a slut, spread rumors that I have sexually transmitted diseases, and said other things that aren't fit to write here. Now boys in my class have joined in, and the torment has gotten worse. And this is just my story. Many other girls at my school are also being harassed and nothing is being done to stop it despite our complaints.

In fact, 8 out of 10 students experience some form of sexual harassment, according to the American Association of University Women study *Hostile Hallways*. Girls who are harassed can go from loving school and being really involved to being afraid to go to class and dropping out of activities. They can lose friends and their grades can suffer. Each student has a right to a harassment-free education, but at our school this right is not being upheld.

As a member of the school board, you know that spreading sexual rumors is a form of sexual harassment and is prohibited by our school district's policy. I'm writing on behalf of a student coalition to ask for your help in stopping harassment at my school by better educating students about our district's policy. The policy has never been explained or printed and distributed to us. If students learn the rules and their rights, it will put a stop to some of the harassment. If conditions at our school don't change, we'll be forced to file a complaint with the federal government.

I would like to set up a time for our student coalition to meet with you as soon as possible to discuss our ideas and how we can work together to make my school harassment free. You can reach me at (your phone number) to schedule a meeting. Thank you for your help.

Sincerely,

Your Name (include your signature above your name)

TIP   If you're writing to your Congressional representative:

When writing to members of Congress, make sure to address them by their full title: "The Honorable (insert full name)." If you're writing to encourage him/her to vote for or against a certain bill, include the full name of the legislation and explain your position. If you're writing for help with a specific issue, research the congressperson's legislative record to see how he/she stands on the issue, or how the problem affects your local community—and its voters.

Speak in Public

To make your campaign successful, you may have to speak before a school board or government officials, at a public rally, during a convention, or, at the very least, at your meetings. If public speaking intimidates you, here are some tips to try:

Get ready. If you have to deliver a speech or are having a meeting with a decision-maker, follow the same steps you'd use to write a call-to-action letter, but include more strong supporting facts or relevant research to build your case. Memorize your speech or talking points so you'll sound interesting, smart, and lively. Be sure to leave your audience with a meaningful or inspirational thought.

Practice, practice, practice. Run through your speech or talking points until you feel comfortable and sound natural. Practice in front of the mirror. Ask your friends, a parent, or your fellow activists to listen and give you advice on how you can win over your audience or make your case.

Dress the part. You want people to listen to your ideas, not critique your outfit. So give some thought to who's in your audience so you can dress appropriately. Most importantly, dress in a way that makes you feel comfortable and confident.

Be confident. People are more likely to listen to you if you look confident and stand tall, with your shoulders back and your head held high (your chin and throat should be at a 90-degree angle).

Know your audience. Your speech can be filled with passion but needs to be backed by facts and respectful to your audience. And just in case your audience knows little about the topic, make sure to explain the basics of the issue clearly so you keep people's interest and attention.

Don't rush. If you're making a speech or talking in front of a group, you might naturally be nervous and start to hurry your words. Take a deep breath before you start. Speak slowly and pronounce your words clearly. Emphasize important words and pause between sentences. All of this takes practice, so just do your best and remember that the more you do it, the more skilled you'll become!

Have some answers. If you're speaking at a public meeting, decision-makers might ask you questions. Prior to your speech, think what you might be asked and how you'll answer. If you or other members of your group don't know how to respond, just say, "I don't have a complete answer to that right now. I can get back to you with one in 24 hours." And then follow up as soon as possible.

Speak from the heart. There may be times when you're unexpectedly called on to talk about your campaign. Even if you don't have any notes in front of you, you can talk about why the issue matters to you and why the audience should care. If you speak from the heart, people will be inspired to listen.

reTroSPecT: WINNING THe VOTe

Women in the United States didn't earn the right to vote until 1920—isn't that crazy? Less than 100 years ago, our opinions were considered unimportant by many male politicians and lawmakers (and this is still the way some people think). Thanks to a relentless campaign by trailblazers like Susan B. Anthony and Elizabeth Cady Stanton, the 19th Amendment to the U.S. Constitution granted women the right to vote. Women can make their voices heard at the ballot box and affect the way the country operates—and now some teens are fighting for the right to vote starting at age 14. Several state legislatures are considering bills being pushed by organizations like the National Youth Rights Association to grant teens "partial" votes (because, obviously, election issues affect the lives of young people, too!). To get involved, go to: www.youthrights.org.

Hold a Peaceful Protest

You have a constitutional right to gather, to organize, and to speak up. Whenever you oppose disrespectful actions, policies, or ideas, you can express your dissatisfaction and take a stand by planning a protest event yourself.

Know your free speech rights. Before you stage a protest, contact your local American Civil Liberties Union (ACLU) to find out your rights and which local and state laws you need to know about. The ACLU also publishes guides about everything from your right to free expression to equality in education. You can find your local office at: www.aclu.org.

Petitions. A petition is a letter signed by hundreds or thousands of people who all support a specific cause. When you're trying to get a decision-maker to listen, numbers count. You can use a petition to get the attention of elected officials, businesses, or influential policymakers. Based on your state's laws, you may also be able to collect signatures to get an issue on a ballot for public office or to call for a vote to kick a politician out of office.

Protest rallies. You can organize a protest rally in a public space, including making a speech about your cause and holding up signs to get your message out to the community and local media. But you can't break any laws (like it could be against the law to block traffic or doorways) during a protest rally, so find out your rights beforehand.

Boycotts and picketing. When a company or business disrespects girls, you can speak with your wallet and boycott the company's products. Advertise your boycott at your school or even through the media (radio, TV, Web). You might also send a letter or petition to the business or picket its headquarters or stores where the products are sold. (Picketing means marching or lining up while holding signs with slogans that spread the word about your cause.)

Promote and Publicize

Making a change might involve getting attention from the media, decision-makers, the community, and girls who are affected by a particular issue. To promote your campaign or get publicity, you can try these ideas:

Make fliers, posters, or pamphlets. Break out the markers, paint, or fancy computer graphic design program and come up with a one-page fact sheet that makes a statement about your campaign. Brainstorm with your group to come up with a slogan or message to catch the attention of your audience. If you're organizing an event, include the "five Ws": **who, what, where, why, when.**

Use the media. The media can be an ally when you need to raise awareness about a problem or get the word out about your campaign. There are lots of organizations that offer advice on how to come up with a media campaign (see pages 213–214). Or enlist the help of your school's journalism advisor or public relations contact (if you have one). Keep these general tips in mind:

- Who is the audience for your campaign and what media will most attract it?

- Once you know the media you want to target, find out who to contact by looking up the email addresses and fax numbers of the media outlet's news director or the appropriate reporters. (Journalists often cover certain topics called "beats," so try to find the reporters who are the best match for your campaign.)

- Write a press release, which is an announcement about your campaign that will pique the interest of the media. Make sure the release includes the five Ws, which a reporter would need to put together an article. (See a sample press release at: www.respectgirls.com.)

You CAN Do It!

The whole "power of one" idea (that one person can make a difference) is really true. To get inspired, read about these amazing girls who stepped up to take the lead and made a huge difference in the process:

- When she was only 12, Mayerly Sanchez of Columbia—a war-torn country where children were fighting for their lives—joined UNICEF's Children's Movement for Peace. Mayerly and other children worked with UNICEF to organize a symbolic special election in 1996 to give children a voice. On that day, a nationwide ceasefire took place, ballot boxes were set out all over the country, and 2.7 million children cast their votes. What did the children of Columbia vote for? Their rights, including freedom of expression and the right to peace and justice. Today, Mayerly continues to educate children in her country.

- Allison Crews had a baby boy when she was in tenth grade. When she was 19, she started www.GirlMom.com to empower other young mothers with an online community where they could find support, read articles about their rights, and get advice on how to pay for college so they might continue their education like she did. Young mothers have written informative features like "Our Rights as Pregnant and Parenting Students" and "A Poor Mama's Guide to Paying for College." Allison not only has created a thriving community but has also been recognized as one of the "Top 30 Under 30 Activists" by Choice USA.

❧ Zimbabwe natives Alexandra and Saunsuray Govere founded the Kijana Project in 2001 to assist AIDS orphans in Africa and to educate youth worldwide about HIV/AIDS. (At the time, Alexandra and Saunsuray weren't even 13 years old.) The girls, who lived in the United States, wanted to provide food, clothing, and books to AIDS orphanages and villages throughout Africa. Today, the sisters' project has grown to include international youth members who publicize the issue of AIDS orphans and create community service projects designed to help them.

These girls might live far from you or may be fighting for causes you've only just learned about, but you still have something in common: You have the power to help spread respect in your community and throughout the world—and to keep living a life that's bold, confident, and totally you.

How Are YOU Getting Respect?

We want to hear your stories about how you stand up for your rights, how you get and give respect in your relationships, and what you're doing to take action to spread respect in your world. Go to www.respectgirls.com to tell us your story and read about amazing girls just like you who are changing our world by fighting for girls' rights and respect for all!

More Info

Here are some of the top resources out there—but this is just a starting point and by no means a complete list. For more resources and for tips on how to find help, resources, or how to research topics further, visit the *Respect* Web site at: www.respectgirls.com.

Helplines

Al-Anon/Alateen
888-4AL-ANON (888-425-2666)
www.al-anon-alateen.org
Support for families and friends of alcoholics. Use the Web site to find a local chapter near you or look it up in the phone book.

America's Pregnancy Helpline
800-672-2296
www.thehelpline.org
Free and confidential help for pregnancy, prenatal health, and reproductive options, including parenting, adoption, and abortion. Check out the Web site for more info and helpful tips on making a decision about pregnancy.

Girls and Boys Town Hotline
800-448-3000
www.girlsandboystown.org
Call anytime with any problem, including feelings of depression or thoughts of suicide. This hotline offers crisis resources and referrals and is staffed by trained counselors.

National Association of Anorexia Nervosa and Associated Disorders
847-831-3438
www.anad.org
Helpline open Monday through Friday 9 A.M. to 5 P.M. (CST). Web site is loaded with information about eating disorders and treatment referrals for your area.

National Center for Victims of Crime
800-FYI-CALL (800-394-2255)
www.ncvc.org/tvp
Offers a toll-free helpline, a comprehensive collection of online resources, and service provider referrals. Check out the center's Teen Victim Project to learn more about assault, bullying, sexual abuse, dating violence, stalking, and how to get help and take action to stop violence against girls.

National Child Abuse Hotline
800-422-4453
www.childhelpusa.org/programs_hotline.htm
A hotline for parents, children, professionals, and anyone concerned that child abuse is occurring.

National Domestic Violence Hotline
800-799-SAFE (800-799-1233)
www.ndvh.org
Crisis intervention, information about domestic violence, and referrals to local service providers for victims and those calling on their behalf.

National Substance Abuse Helpline
800-DRUG-HELP (800-378-4435)
A confidential helpline for help with questions or concerns related to substance abuse.

Rape, Abuse and Incest National Network (RAINN) National Sexual Assault Hotline
800-656-4673
www.rainn.org
This free, confidential counseling hotline is available 24/7. The Web site has tons of information about sexual abuse and what to do if you've been sexually assaulted.

SAFE (Self-Abuse Finally Ends)
800-DONT-CUT (800-366-8288)
Get referrals to local programs that can help girls who self-injure or cut.

Teen Relationships Hotline
800-799-SAFE (800-799-7233)
www.teenrelationships.org
Call the nationwide 24-hour hotline for support, assistance, information, counseling, shelter, and other services. The Web-based chat room is open Monday, Tuesday, and Wednesday evenings.

Abuse, Mental Health, and Counseling

American Psychological Association
www.apa.org
Wondering if shyness is normal, if you're getting enough sleep, if your perfectionism is harmful, or how to tell if you have depression? Learn about post-traumatic stress disorder and other mental and emotional traumas, and how to find a therapist in your state.

National Association of Social Workers (NASW)
www.naswdc.org
You can do an online search of the NASW Register of Clinical Social Workers to find a social worker in your area who can provide mental health services.

U.S. Department of Justice: Office on Violence Against Women
202-307-6026
www.ojp.usdoj.gov/vawo
Handles the Department's legal and policy issues regarding violence against women, including responding to requests for information. Works closely with state, tribal, and local jurisdictions to implement the mandates of the Violence Against Women Act and subsequent legislation.

V-Day
www.vday.org
Nonprofit corporation that distributes funds to grassroots, national, and international organizations and programs that work to stop violence against women and girls.

The Courage to Heal: A Guide for Women Survivors of Child Sexual Abuse by Ellen Bass and Laura Davis (New York: Perennial Currents, 1994). This book offers advice, resources, and practical guidance for sexual abuse victims on getting help and building self-esteem. Plus, it recommends supportive strategies for families and friends.

In Love and in Danger: A Teen's Guide to Breaking Free of Abusive Relationships by Barrie Levy (Washington, DC: Seal Press, 1998). A guide designed to help with numerous relationship issues.

Surviving a Stalker: Everything You Need to Know to Keep Yourself Safe by Linden Gross (New York: Marlowe & Company, 2000). From the founder of Stalking Victims Sanctuary, this book covers everything from cyber stalking to creating safety plans. Or see: www.stalkingvictims.com.

When Nothing Matters Anymore: A Survival Guide for Depressed Teens by Bev Cobain (Minneapolis: Free Spirit Publishing, 1998). A book for teens on how to recognize depression, get help, and stay well.

When Something Feels Wrong: A Survival Guide About Abuse for Young People by Deanna S. Pledge (Minneapolis: Free Spirit Publishing, 2002). Support and healing for teens on physical, sexual, and emotional abuse. Checklists, journaling exercises, and encouragement help the healing process.

Body and Health

About Face
www.about-face.org
Check out the Make Changes section for advice on
how to improve your body image and speaking up to
companies that promote dangerous body ideals.

The Body Positive
510-548-0101
www.thebodypositive.org
Teaches girls how to develop a better body image and healthy relationships with food.

Club Drugs
www.clubdrugs.org
Learn about the latest club drugs and the negative effects they can have on your mind and
body. A service of the National Institute on Drug Abuse.

gURL
www.gurl.com
Find out how your brain and body work—including dealing with tough emotions, health,
sex, relationships, and body choices.

National Eating Disorders Association
206-382-3587
www.nationaleatingdisorders.org
Get information on all forms of eating disorders and treatment, and get referrals for doctors,
counselors, nutritionists, and facilities in your area.

Teen Health
www.teenhealth.org
Articles, answers, facts, and advice on everything related to your health—physical, mental,
and sexual.

WebMD
www.webmd.com
If there's one Web site that has it all about your mind and body, it's WebMD. Using its
search engine, you can find excellent information on anything from depression, to emergency contraception, to self-injury. When searching, be sure to check out the WebMD Search
Results first (before you go clicking around links provided by sponsors).

Women's Sports Foundation
800-227-3988
www.womenssportsfoundation.org
Find out about every sport under the sun and how to get involved, and learn about athletic
scholarships. Check out the GoGirlGo! section to read about girl sports stars.

Adios, Barbie: Young Women Write About Body Image and Identity by Ophira Edut (Washington, DC: Seal Press, 1998). A celebration of the fact that female bodies come in all shapes, sizes, and colors. Plus, stories of body outlaws who don't conform to unhealthy norms.

The Beauty Myth: How Images of Beauty Are Used Against Women by Naomi Wolf (New York: Perennial, 2002). Feminist Naomi Wolf argues that women's insecurities are made worse and then exploited by the cosmetic, diet, and plastic surgery industries. And then girls spend all their time obsessing over their looks instead of other important issues, like self-respect.

The Body Project: An Intimate History of American Girls by Joan Jacobs Brumberg (New York: Vintage, 1997). Starting with a statistic that 53 percent of girls are dissatisfied with their bodies, the book looks at "why?" Brumberg combs through girls' diaries dating from 1830 to the present day and explains why now more than ever girls' main projects are their bodies.

Deal With It! A Whole New Approach to Body, Brain, and Life as a Gurl by Esther Drill, Heather McDonald, and Rebecca Odes (New York: Pocket Books, 1999). The ultimate guide for all things girls have to deal with, from understanding feelings to sex and how your body is changing. It'll suck you in because it's so cool, straightforward, and real, and because it has tons of resource listings and illustrations.

Easy for You to Say: Q & As for Teens Living with Chronic Illness or Disability by Miriam Kaufman (Tonawanda, NY: Firefly Books, 1995). Written in a Q&A format, this book tackles the concerns of teens with chronic illness or disability. Subjects include, family, sexuality, friends, and dating.

Phenomenal Woman: Four Poems Celebrating Women by Maya Angelou (New York: Random House, 1995). Four inspirational and empowering poems, including "Phenomenal Woman," about loving the female form.

A Very Hungry Girl: How I Filled Up on Life . . . and How You Can, Too! by Jessica Weiner (Carlsbad, CA: How House Inc., 2003). A personal look at how all girls want to be loved, feel worthy, and fit in. Find out how Jessica figured this out for herself amid a long battle with eating disorders and low self-esteem.

Education and Learning

American Association of University Women (AAUW)
800-326-AAUW (800-326-2289)
www.aauw.org
Promotes equity, lifelong education, and positive societal change for all women and girls.

Ms. Foundation for Women
212-742-2300
www.ms.foundation.org
Funds projects that nurture girls' leadership skills, including Take Our Daughters and Sons to Work Day.

National Center for Learning Disabilities
212-545-7510
www.ncld.org
Information on learning disabilities and what help is available.

The Safe Schools Coalition
866-HF-ZONE-1 (866-439-6631) Crisis Phone
206-632-0622 business phone
www.safeschoolscoalition.org
A public-private partnership in support of gay, lesbian, bisexual, and transgender youth. Ofers resources as a starting point for educators, parents/guardians, and youth. The Crisis Phone is available 24/7.

Transitions Abroad
802-442-4827
www.transitionsabroad.com
Learn all about studying- or volunteering- abroad programs for teens.

The Teenage Liberation Handbook: How to Quit School and Get a Real Life and Education by Grace Llewellyn (Halifax, Canada: Lowry House, 1998). For the motivated girl who doesn't like learning in the school environment, this inspiring classic has everything you need to know to "unschool" yourself and take charge of your education, including tips on how to talk to your parents about changing your education and Web resources that support your self-schooling adventure.

The Teenagers' Guide to School Outside the Box by Rebecca Greene (Minneapolis: Free Spirit Publishing, 2001). How to explore non-traditional education experiences from internships, to volunteering, to studying abroad.

Where Do I Go from Here? by Esther Drill, Rebecca Odes, and Heather McDonald (New York: Penguin, 2004). From the creators of Gurl.com, this book discusses the many different types of post–high school experiences—from college, to volunteering, to taking a year off—to help you figure out where you might be happiest and alternative ways to learn.

Equal Rights

American Civil Liberties Union (ACLU)
www.aclu.org
The ACLU defends the civil liberties of all people. Check the Web site for phone numbers of local offices in your state.

Amnesty International
212-807-8400
www.amnestyusa.org/youth
Fights for human rights worldwide and offers guidance and training for young activists.

Feminist Majority Foundation (FMF)
703-522-2214
www.feminist.org
Dedicated to women's and girls' equality, this organization's Web site has tons of news and resources on issues that affect women's rights and how to get involved.

Gay & Lesbian Alliance Against Defamation (GLAAD)
212-629-3322
www.glaad.org
Works to promote and ensure fair, accurate, and inclusive representation of GLBTQ people and events in all forms of media. The Web site includes articles and resources on GLBTQ rights.

International Network for Girls (INfG)
www.girlsrights.org
The INfG focuses on improving girls' rights around the world by advocating for countries to honor the Platform for Action adopted at the 1995 Beijing Women's Conference, which specifically outline girls' rights around the world.

National Association for the Advancement of Colored People (NAACP)
877-NAACP-98 (877-622-2798)
www.naacp.org
Adult and youth members throughout the United States and the world are advocates for civil rights in their communities and monitor political, educational, social, and economic equality.

National Organization for Women (NOW)
202-628-8669
www.now.org
A watchdog organization for women's rights and equality. Go to the Web site to learn about issues that concern girls, and your rights and how to protect them.

National Women's Hall of Fame
315-568-8060
www.greatwomen.org
This organization's Web site is a searchable shrine to some of the greatest women in U.S. history who made contributions to the arts, athletics, business, education, government, the humanities, philanthropy, and science.

National Youth Rights Association
301-738-6769
www.youthrights.org
Dedicated to defending the civil and human rights of young people in the United States. This organization aims to achieve its goals through educating people about youth rights, working with public officials to devise fitting policy solutions to problems affecting young people, and empowering young people to work on their own behalf.

Third Wave Foundation
212-675-0700
www.thirdwavefoundation.org
Fights for the equality of all—regardless of age, gender, race, sexual orientation, economic status, and level of education. Supports the leadership of young women 15 to 30 by providing resources, public education, and networking opportunities.

U.S. Equal Employment Opportunity Commission (EEOC)—See listing under "Sexual Harassment and Bullying."

33 Things Every Girl Should Know About Women's History: From Suffragettes to Skirt Lengths to the E.R.A. edited by Tonya Bolden (New York: Crown Books, 2002). Find out how revolutionary women fought for equal rights so you can, too.

Manifesta: Young Women, Feminism, and the Future by Jennifer Baumgardner and Amy Richards (New York: Farrar, Straus and Giroux, 2000). This call to arms describes the "seven deadly sins" the media commits against feminism, calls for urgent activism by young women, and talks about what a world with equality would look like.

The Second Sex by Simone de Beauvoir. (New York: Vintage, 1989). This 1949 classic explores how one "becomes" a woman. The book flap says it all: "The classic manifesto of the liberated woman, this book explores every facet of a woman's life."

To Be Real: Telling the Truth and Changing the Face of Feminism edited by Rebecca Walker (New York: Anchor Books, 1995). With essays by men and women, this is an exploration of modern-day feminism and its impact on everyday life and the future.

Family

The Children's Rights Council
301-559-3120
www.gocrc.com
This national organization helps kids have meaningful and safe contact with both parents and extended family.

GirlMom
www.girlmom.com
Community forums, articles, and encouragement for teen moms.

Stepfamily Network
www.stepfamily.net
Get support and advice on dealing with stepparents.

Bringing Up Parents: The Teenager's Handbook by Alex J. Packer (Minneapolis: Free Spirit Publishing, 1993). Tips for how teens can resolve conflicts, create trust, and improve their relationships with parents.

Cool Communication: From Conflict to Cooperation for Parents and Kids by Andrea Frank Henkart and Journey Henkart (New York: Perigee Books, 2002). A mother and her teen daughter write about keeping it real with great communication skills. This is a must-have book if you want to have a mutually respectful relationship with your parents.

Dads and Daughters: How to Inspire, Understand, and Support Your Daughter by Joe Kelly (New York: Broadway, 2003). If your dad isn't spending enough time with you or you just aren't relating, you'll both appreciate this book. Or, check out the Web site at: www. dadsanddaughters.org.

The Grieving Teen: A Guide for Teenagers and Their Friends by Helen Fitzgerald (New York: Fireside, 2000). This book includes FAQs that teens have about grief, followed by a What You Can Do section. The topics covered include death from AIDS, post-traumatic stress disorder, Internet support, and more.

Media

Angelfire
www.angelfire.com
Learn how to build your own Web site and host it for free.
This site has everything you need to get started, including
a step-by-step beginner's guide.

Blogger
www.blogger.com
A blog gives you your own voice on the Web. Learn how to create your own blog so you can
publish your thoughts, writing, or stories about the real lives of girls.

Center for Media Literacy
310-581-0260
www.medialit.org
Nonprofit educational organization that provides leadership, public education, professional
development, and educational resources nationally. Works to help citizens, especially the
young, develop critical thinking and media-production skills needed to live fully in the 21st
century media culture.

The Girls, Women + Media Project
www.mediaandwomen.org
Examines how pop culture and media represent, affect, employ, and serve girls, and how
you can take action to promote responsibility and respect. Plus, the site includes tons of
resources to learn more about girls and the media.

Listen Up!
212-725-7000
www.pbs.org/merrow/listenup
A youth media network that connects young video producers to resources, support, and
projects in the field to help create an authentic youth voice in the media.

Wiretap
415-284-1420
www.alternet.org/wiretapmag
An independent news source by and for socially conscious youth.

Youth Entertainment Studios (YES)
757-545-8766
www.yesamerica.org
Gives teens a safe place to develop their own media, including music, video, Web, and print
productions. YES works with communities nationwide and offers summer camps.

Branded: The Buying and Selling of Teenagers by Alissa Quart (New York: Basic Books, 2003). How companies bombard teens with marketing that "saps them of individuality and imagination" to get them to not only buy products, but be products.

Can't Buy My Love: How Advertising Changes the Way We Think and Feel (New York: Touchstone, 1999) and *Deadly Persusasion: Why Women and Girls Must Fight the Addictive Power of Advertising* (New York: Free Press, 1999) by Jean Kilbourne. Both books expose how advertising negatively shapes the way girls and women feel about themselves, what they want, and the way they treat themselves. See the author's Web site for more resources: www.jeankilbourne.com.

Ms. magazine
www.msmagazine.com
Launched in 1971, *Ms.* was founded by feminist icons such as Gloria Steinem and Pat Carbine. Today the magazine is still outspoken and doesn't just *write* about girls' and women's struggles for equality and political power, but leads them to take action.

Teen Voices magazine
www.teenvoices.com
This magazine, written by and for teen girls, is all about building respect from the inside out. Visit the Web site to learn about how to contribute an article.

Where the Girls Are: Growing Up Female with the Mass Media by Susan J. Douglas (New York: Three Rivers Press, 1995). A look at how American media has portrayed women over the past 50 years.

Relationships and Sex

American Social Health Association (ASHA)
www.ashastd.org
Provides clear instructions for how to use both female and male condoms, and facts about STDs. Recommended by the Centers for Disease Control and Prevention (CDC).

Planned Parenthood Federation of America (PPFA)
800-230-7526
www.plannedparenthood.org
Nationwide, PPFA provides comprehensive reproductive and complementary health care services in settings that preserve and protect the privacy and rights of girls. You can call the 800 number to ask questions or schedule an appointment with a clinic near you. Their Web site offers reliable information about sex, pregnancy, and more.

Scarleteen
www.scarleteen.com
Offers big-sister advice on relationships, sexuality, sexual intimacy, building trust, communicating, and strategies for appreciating your body.

Sex, Etc.
www.sxetc.org
The name pretty much says it all. Written by teens for teens (and sponsored by Rutgers Unviersity) this site provides practical sex info and covers many other topics, including relationships, emotional health, and abuse. Check out "The Roadmap: A Teen Guide to Changing Your School's Sex Ed."

Sexuality Information & Education Council of the United States (SIECUS)
212-819-9770
www.siecus.org
A diverse clearinghouse for information about sexuality education, sexual health, and sexual rights programs.

Teen Wire
www.teenwire.com
Offers great advice on family matters, friendships, relationships, and sexual choices and health. Sponsored by Planned Parenthood Federation of America.

When Love Hurts
www.dvirc.org.au/whenlove/index.htm
A teen girl's online guide to creating respectful romantic relationships. Includes true stories, abuse and respect checklists, and advice on how to break up.

Changing Bodies, Changing Lives: A Book for Teens on Sex and Relationships by Ruth Bell (New York: Three Rivers Press, 1998). Written by the authors of the classic book that your mom probably read, *Our Bodies, Ourselves,* this book thoroughly covers relationships, sex, and sexuality—the emotional and physical issues and risks.

Dating with Confidence: A Teen's Survival Guide by Jacqueline Jarosz (Avon, MA: Adams Media, 2000). How to know if you're ready to date and how to deal with all the related dating dilemmas, like dates on a budget and first date do's and don'ts.

GLBTQ: The Survival Guide for Queer and Questioning Teens by Kelly Huegel (Minneapolis: Free Spirit Publishing, 2003). Advice, true stories, and resources for exploring gay, lesbian, bisexual and transgender relationships, dating, and more.

The Go Ask Alice Book of Answers: A Guide to Good Physical, Sexual, and Emotional Health by Columbia University's Health Education Program (New York: Henry Holt & Company, 1998). Based on the popular Web site by the same name, get answers to questions about your body, sex, and emotional well-being.

Slut! Growing Up Female with a Bad Reputation by Leora Tanenbaum (New York: Perennial, 2000). Get behind the real meaning of how girls and others are using the word "slut"—and what to do about it.

Self-Defense

Dr. Ruthless
www.dr-ruthless.com
Get a look at impact self-defense and find inspiration for taking a course. Also has a helpful collection of informative articles and survival tips.

Impact Bay Area (formerly BAMM)
510-208-0474
www.impactbayarea.org
A great overview of impact-style self-defense and links to impact self-defense offerings in other states and countries.

Impact Self-Defense
800-345-5425
www.prepareinc.com
Find a program near you.

YMCA—See listing under "Sisterhood and Mentoring."
www.ymca.org
At work in more than 120 countries around the world, serving more than 45 million people. Programs may vary by branch.

YWCA—See listing under "Sisterhood and Mentoring."
Many YWCAs offer self-defense courses. Check listings in your area.

Beauty Bites Beast: Awakening the Warrior Within Women and Girls by Ellen B. Snortland (Pasadena, CA: Trilogy Books, 1998). A great introduction to the mindset of self-defense. Teaches assertiveness and self-defense skills.

Girl Power: Self-Defense for Teens by Burt Konzak, Melina Konzak, and Sonya Konzak (Toronto, Canada: Sports Books Publisher, 1999). Read about situations that many teens encounter in their daily lives and learn preventive measures, avoidance techniques, and self-defense skills.

Self-Worth

Be True to Yourself: A Daily Guide for Teenage Girls by Amanda Ford (Berkeley, CA: Conari Press, 2000). In 365 one-page essays written by teen Amanda Ford, you'll get advice and insight on dating, drinking, self-worth, fights with friends, dealing with parents, and more.

Blue Jean: What Young Women Are Thinking, Saying, and Doing by Sherry S. Handel (Rochester, NY: Blue Jean Press, 2001). A grab bag of essays written by teen girls and young women on everything from volunteering and activism, to why girls shy away from the feminism movement, to attention deficit disorder, to creating your own zine or movie.

Don't Give It Away! A Workbook of Self-Awareness and Self-Affirmations for Young Women by Iyanla Vanzant (New York: Fireside, 1999). Iyanla was a teen mom and high school dropout, and she went through a lot of family traumas and abuse as a child. But today she's helping young women find and keep their power. In this workbook, you can express your thoughts and feelings about the things that matter to you, and learn to find the love you want by loving yourself first.

Ophelia Speaks: Adolescent Girls Write About Their Search for Self by Sara Shandler (New York: Harper Collins, 1999). An "answer" to the book *Reviving Ophelia,* this collection of writings from girls 12 to 18 explores the challenges that girls are facing today, including body image, family, friends, and sexuality.

Real Girl/Real World: Tools for Finding Your True Self by Heather M. Gray and Samantha Phillips (Seattle: Seal Press, 1998). Learn how to make choices you're comfortable with and explore a wide range of topics, including body image, nutrition, safe sex, and more.

Reviving Ophelia: Saving the Selves of Adolescent Girls by Mary Pipher (New York: Ballantine Books, 1994). A truthful look at the "girl-poisoning" culture that turns independent-spirited young girls into struggling teens who have low self-worth and self-respect.

Revolution from Within: A Book of Self-Esteem by Gloria Steinem (New York: Little, Brown, 1993). Feminist icon Gloria Steinem writes about self-worth, the importance of unlearning unhealthy beliefs, knowing the difference between romance and love, and so much more. It's written for women, but you can handle her straightforward, mature tone, right?

Schoolgirls: Young Women, Self Esteem, and the Confidence Gap by Peggy Orenstein (New York: Anchor Books, 1995). Inspired by a study from the AAUW Women that shows girls' self-esteem plummeting as they reach adolescence, this book goes inside two different schools in northern California where girls struggle for equal educations, assertiveness, and confidence.

What Do You Really Want? How to Set a Goal and Go for It! by Beverly K. Bachel (Minneapolis: Free Spirit, 2001). A step-by-step guide to goal-setting and planning written just for teens.

Sexual Harassment and Bullying

The Empower Program
202-686-1908
www.empowered.org
Works with teens to end the culture of violence and cruelty that includes bullying, rumors, fights, cliques, and more.

Equal Rights Advocates (ERA)
800-839-4ERA (800-839-4372)
www.equalrights.org
The ERA protects equal rights and economic opportunities for women and girls through litigation and advocacy. Free, 24/7 legal advice and counseling about sexual harassment and discrimination at school or work.

The Gay, Lesbian and Straight Education Network
212-727-0135
www.glsen.org
Works to ensure safe schools for all students by taking action against anti-LGBT bullying. Get involved by telling your story or joining a campaign.

National Women's Law Center
202-588-5180
www.nwlc.org
Get advice on how to advocate for a sexual harassment policy at your school and fight for other educational rights.

U.S. Department of Education: Office for Civil Rights (OCR)
800-USA-LEARN (800-872-5327)
www.ed.gov
Learn your education rights and how to file a sexual harassment or discrimination complaint.

U.S. Equal Employment Opportunity Commission: Youth at Work
800-669-4000
www.youth.eeoc.gov
Learn your rights at work and how to file a sexual harassment or discrimination complaint.

Sexual Harassment: What Teens Should Know by Carol Rust Nash (Berkeley Heights, NJ: Enslow Publishers, 1996). Covers sexual harassment in all its angles, the effects it has on its victims, and guidelines for confronting the harasser.

Sisterhood and Mentors

Boys and Girls Clubs of America (BGCA)
404-487-5700
www.bgca.org
With locations nationwide, BGCA offers confidence-building programs focused on your future, character, leadership, health, athletics, and the arts.

Girls For A Change (GFC)
408-515-8147
www.girlsforachange.org
Matches women mentors with girls who develop social change projects to transform their communities, learn leadership skills, and strengthen their sisterhood.

Girls Inc.
800-374-4475
www.girlsinc.org
Dedicated to inspiring all girls to be strong, smart, and bold, and to prepare them to lead successful, independent, and fulfilling lives. The Web site has a great reading list and resources. Check out the Girls' Bill of Rights.

Girl Scouts of the U.S.A.
800-478-7248
www.girlscouts.org
With chapters nationwide, the Girls Scouts helps girls ages 5 to 17 build self-worth, values, leadership skills, and a bunch of other important skills through meetings, activities, trips, and volunteer work.

International Order of Rainbow Girls
918-423-1328
www.iorg.org
This nondenominational organization helps girls ages 11 to 20 build leadership and speaking skills and promotes confidence, sisterhood, and charity. Girls are elected to office by their peers to run the local chapters' meetings, business, and events, which include dances, fundraisers, and extended trips.

YMCA
www.ymca.com
The largest nonprofit community service organization in America, working to meet the health and social service needs of 18.9 million men, women, and children in 10,000 communities in the United States. Ys are for people of all faiths, races, abilities, ages, and incomes. The YMCA's strength is in the people it brings together.

YWCA
800-YWCA-US1 (800-992-2871)
www.ywca.org
With more than 25 million members around the globe, the organization's mission is to "eliminate racism and empower women." The YWCA provides safe places for women and girls, builds strong girl leaders, and advocates for women's rights and civil rights in Congress.

How to Say No and Keep Your Friends: Peer Pressure Reversal for Teens and Preteens by Sharon Scott (Amherst, MA: HRD Press, 1997). Keep that respect flowing by learning to set boundaries with your friends.

Odd Girl Speaks Out: Girls Write About Bullies, Cliques, Popularity, and Jealousy by Rachel Simmons (Orlando, FL: Harcourt Books, 2004). Poems, songs, confessions, and essays from girls about in-fighting among girls and how to stop it.

Teen Girlfriends: Celebrating the Good Times, Getting Through the Hard Times by Julia DeVillers (Berkeley, CA: Wildcat Canyon Press, 2001). A look at why our friendships are so important and how to keep them healthy and strong.

Social Activism

Ask Amy
www.feminist.com/askamy
You can ask questions about your rights and how to be an activist, and find out more about issues that affect girls. Check out Amy's Most Asked Questions to get started.

Contact Congress Members
www.house.gov/writerep
Find the name of your Congressperson and you can even send an email from this site, or learn where to send a letter.

Do Something
www.dosomething.org
Grants for young people who are leading projects to change their communities. Plus, the organization creates a cool magazine with advice on how to "do something" and success stories.

E the People
646-536-9305
www.e-thepeople.org
Free, nonpartisan public forum where you can talk politics and connect with lawmakers nationwide.

Idea List
212-843-3973
www.idealist.org
Resources for starting social change projects and organizations started by other young people who are making a difference.

National Council of Women's Organizations
202-293-4505
www.womensorganizations.org
A nonpartisan, nonprofit umbrella organization of almost 200 groups that represent more than 10 million women across the United States. You can learn about organizations already taking action and how you can join them.

National Youth Rights Association—See listing under "Equal Rights."
www.youthrights.org

Take the Lead
413-538-2409
www.mtholyoke.edu/offices/comm/takethelead
Offers a weekend designed for idealistic, action-oriented young women from across the country who want to make a difference in the world. Participate in fun, interactive workshops and activities that build leadership skills and come up with your own action project.

UNICEF: Voices of Youth
www.unicef.org/voy
Communication skills for young activists, including letter writing, public speaking, event planning, creating posters and leaflets, and dealing with the media.

Women's Human Rights Net
www.whrnet.org
Tools, news, resources, and organization listings for how getting involved in the fight for girls' rights.

Youth Action Net
410-951-1500
www.youthactionnet.org
Launched by the International Youth Foundation (IYF), this is a place for young adults to connect with each other to make a difference in their communities.

Grassroots: A Field Guide for Feminist Activism
by Jennifer Baumgardner and Amy Richards
(New York: Farrar, Straus, and Giroux, 2005).
This inspiring book will help you find your voice, organize your community, and get involved.

The Kid's Guide to Social Action: How to Solve the Social Problems You Choose—and Turn Creative Thinking into Positive Action by Barbara A. Lewis (Minneapolis: Free Spirit Publishing, 1998). Step-by-step instructions show how to write letters, do interviews, make speeches, take surveys, raise funds, get media coverage, and more. Forms to create petitions, proclamations, and news releases are included.

Teens Take It to Court: Young People Who Challenged the Law—and Changed Your Life by Thomas A. Jacobs (Minneapolis: Free Spirit Publishing, 2006). Learn how teens turned their power into social action and changed the law.

Teen Power Politics: Make Yourself Heard by Sara Jane Boyers (Brookfield, CT: Millbrook Press, 2000). How you can figure out what you stand for, get organized, or join an activism movement. Includes true stories about teen activists and resources.

Notes

Chapter 2: Your Mind

1. *Girls' Rights: Conducted for Girls Incorporated* (Harris Interactive Inc., 2000).

Chapter 3: Your Body

1. *Age Distribution: Cosmetic Patients 18 or Younger* (American Society of Plastic Surgeons, 2004).

2. and 3. *Youth Risk Behavior Survey* (Centers for Disease Control and Prevention, 2003).

4. Smolak, L., *Next Door Neighbor's Puppet Guidebook* (National Eating Disorders Association, 1996).

5. Wolf, Naomi, *The Beauty Myth: How Images of Beauty Are Used Against Women* (Perennial, 2002), 185.

6. NEDA Statistics: "Eating Disorders and Their Precursors" (National Eating Disorders Association, 1995).

7. Wolf, 187–188, 199.

8. and 9. *Youth Risk Behavior Survey,* 2003.

10. Strong, Marilee, *A Bright Red Scream: Self-Mutilation and the Language of Pain* (New York: Penguin, 1998), 25.

11. NEDA "Eating Disorders" Statistics.

Chapter 4: Your Media IQ

1. "Facts About Marketing to Children," www.newdream.org/kids/facts.php (New American Dream, 2005).

2. Thomsen, Steven R., Michelle M. Weber, and Lora Beth Brown, "The Relationship Between Health and Fitness Magazine Reading and Eating-Disordered Weight-Loss Methods Among High School Girls," *American Journal of Health Education,* vol. 32 (2001), 133–138.

3. Jernigan, D.H., J. Ostroff, C. Ross, and J.A. O'Hara, "Sex Differences in Adolescent Exposure to Alcohol Advertising in Magazines," Archives of Pediatric and Adolescent Medicine, vol. 158 (July 2004), 629–634.

4. Signorielli, Nancy, *Reflections of Girls in the Media: A Two-Part Study on Gender and Media* (Children Now and the Kaiser Family Foundation with the University of Delaware, April 1997).

5. Lauzen, Martha M., *Boxed In: Women on Screen and Behind the Scenes in the 2000–2001 Prime-Time Season* (San Diego State University, 2001).

6. Signorielli.

7. Kunkel, Dale, Kirstie Cope, Wendy Jo Maynard Farinola, Erica Biely, Emma Rollin, and Edward Donnerstein, *Sex on TV: A Biennial Report to the Kaiser Family Foundation* (University of California at Santa Barbara, 1999).

8. "Watching Sex on Television Predicts Adolescent Initiation of Sexual Behavior," *Pediatrics* (September 2004).

9. Grossman, Dave, and Gloria DeGaetano, *Stop Teaching Our Kids to Kill: A Call to Action Against TV, Movie, and Video Game Violence* (Crown Media, 1999), 323–337.

Chapter 7: Relationships

1. "1848 Declaration of Sentiments Seneca Falls," www.womensrightsfriendsforever.org/declaration1848.html (Friends of Women's Rights National Park, Inc.).

Chapter 8: Sex

1. *Teens Today* (Students Against Destructive Decisions and Liberty Mutual Group, 2003).

2. and 3. *Youth Risk Behavior Survey,* 2003.

4. and 5. *Girls and Sexual Health Fact Sheet* (Girls Inc. National Resource Center, 2001).

6. and 7. *America's Adults and Teens Sound Off About Teen Pregnancy: An Annual National Survey* (National Campaign to Prevent Teen Pregnancy, 2003).

8. "National Survey of Teens About Sex: Gender Roles" (The Kaiser Family Foundation and *Seventeen,* 2002).

9. *Pregnancy 14 and Younger: The Sexual Behavior of Young Adolescents* (National Campaign to Prevent Teen Pregnancy, 2003).

Chapter 9: Dealing with Abuse

1. Heise, Lori, Mary Ellsberg, and Megan Gottemoeller, "Ending Violence Against Women," *Population Reports,* series L (Johns Hopkins University School of Public Health, Population Information Program, 1999).

2. *Female Genital Mutilation—A Human Rights Information Pack* (Amnesty International, 1997).

3. Heise, et al.

4. *Abuse and Teens* (The Empower Program, sponsored by Liz Claiborne Inc. and conducted by Knowledge Networks, Social Control, Verbal Abuse, and Violence Among Teenagers, December 2000).

5. *Violence by Intimates: Analysis of Data on Crimes by Current or Former Spouses, Boyfriends, and Girlfriends* (U.S. Department of Justice, March 1998).

6. *Child Sexual Abuse Fact Sheet: Incest* (National Center for Victims of Crime, 2004).

7. Darroch, Jacqueline E., David J. Landry, and Selene Oslak, "Age Differences Between Sexual Partners in the United States," *Family Planning Perspectives,* vol. 31, July/August 1999.

Chapter 10: Defending Yourself

1. *National Crime Victimization Survey* (Bureau of Justice Statistics, U.S. Department of Justice, 2000).

2. Bandura, Albert, and Elizabeth M. Ozer, "Mechanisms Governing Empowerment Effects: A Self-Efficacy Analysis," *Journal of Personality and Social Psychology,* vol. 58 (March 1990), 472–486.

Chapter 11: Fighting for Your Rights at School

1. and 2. *Hostile Hallways: Bullying, Teasing, and Sexual Harassment in School* (Harris Interactive, Inc., sponsored by the American Association of University Women, 2002).

Index

About the Authors

Courtney Macavinta and Andrea Vander Pluym are award-winning writers who both got their start in journalism on their high school newspapers. Their collaboration began on the creative leadership team at ChickClick, a ground-breaking online and radio network that served over a million girls and women.

Courtney is an investigative journalist whose articles have been syndicated by the Associated Press and published by the *Washington Post, Wired News, Red Herring, Business 2.0,* and the *Sacramento Bee* online. For several years she was a political reporter for CNET News.com, where she covered the first Supreme Court hearing on Internet free speech and interviewed newsmakers. Fighting for young women's empowerment has always been Courtney's passion. Until 2001, she was the editorial director of ChickClick, where she oversaw publishing and helped relaunch the network to cover topics such as body image, health, and getting into college. In 2002 Courtney received a Fund for Investigative Journalism grant to investigate women's working conditions in Silicon Valley, and she has appeared on radio, TV, and in national print media as an expert on subjects from women's media to politics. She has collaborated or volunteered with Girls For A Change, the YMCA, CanTeen, Our Schools, Our Media, the Ms. Foundation's Take Our Daughters and Sons to Work Day, and Planned Parenthood Federation of America's teenwire.com. Courtney lives in San Jose, California, with her husband.

Andrea is the author of *What Should I Do?*, an advice book for pre-teen girls. Her articles and columns have appeared in *Teen, Planet Girl, Shape, Variety, Los Angeles View,* and other publications. After struggling with the messages mainstream teen media was giving to girls, Andrea dedicated herself to supporting girls in getting honest and real advice about their bodies, minds, and futures. In 1999, she joined ChickClick, where she launched new content including teen essays and fiction and oversaw daily production as managing editor. Andrea has also lectured on writing for teens at national conferences, including those hosted by the Society of Children's Book Writers and Illustrators. She volunteers as an assistant instructor for teen self-defense workshops, and has volunteered with Bay Area Teen Voices, Girls in the Hall, and GirlVentures. Andrea lives in the San Francisco Bay area with her family.

Other Great Books from Free Spirit

The Teen Survival Guide to Dating & Relating
Real-World Advice for Teens on Guys, Girls, Growing Up, and Getting Along
by Annie Fox, M.Ed. (also known as Hey Terra!)
The creator of an award-winning Web site helps teens and young adults build healthier relationships with everyone in their lives—including themselves. For ages 13 & up.
$15.95; 256 pp.; softcover; illus.; 7¼" x 9¼"

GLBTQ*
The Survival Guide for Queer & Questioning Teens
* Gay, Lesbian, Bisexual, Transgender, Questioning
by Kelly Huegel
A helpful look at the challenges and issues gay, lesbian, bisexual, transgender, and questioning teens face at school, at home, and with friends. Recommended for any GLBTQ teen—and for any straight friend, parent, teacher, or other adult who cares and wants to understand. For ages 13 & up.
$15.95; 240 pp.; softcover; 6" x 9"

What Do You Really Want?
How to Set a Goal and Go for It! A Guide for Teens
by Beverly K. Bachel with a special note from polar explorer Ann Bancroft
This book is a step-by-step guide to goal setting, written especially for teens. Each chapter includes fun, creative exercises, practical tips, words of wisdom from famous "goal-getters," real-life examples from teens, and success stories. Includes reproducibles. For ages 11 & up.
$12.95; 144 pp.; softcover; illus.; 6" x 9"

Boy v. Girl?
How Gender Shapes Who We Are, What We Want, and How We Get Along
by George Abrahams, Ph.D., and Sheila Ahlbrand
What does it really mean to be a boy or a girl? This book invites young readers to examine gender roles and stereotypes, overcome gender barriers, and be themselves. Written for both boys and girls, *Boy v. Girl?* explores the issues and examines the facts—about hormones, history, laws, and more. It encourages readers to learn who they are, imagine what they can be—and get past those things that get in the way. For ages 10–15.
$14.95; 208 pp.; softcover; illus.; 7" x 9"

To place an order or to request a free catalog of SELF-HELP FOR KIDS® and SELF-HELP FOR TEENS® materials, please write, call, email, or visit our Web site:

Free Spirit Publishing Inc.
217 Fifth Avenue North • Suite 200 • Minneapolis, MN 55401-1299
toll-free 800.735.7323 • local 612.338.2068 • fax 612.337.5050
help4kids@freespirit.com • www.freespirit.com